THE NATURE OF
FROGS

HARRY PARSONS

THE NATURE OF
FROGS

AMPHIBIANS WITH

ATTITUDE

GREYSTONE BOOKS

Douglas & McIntyre Publishing Group

Vancouver/Toronto/New York

To Dr. Francis Cook, who let a 12-year-old explore the Herpetology Collection of the National Museum of Natural Sciences that winter afternoon in Ottawa, Ontario. To Don Rivard and Dr. Don Smith for giving me a chance to earn something resembling a living in herpetology. To Dr. Cook and Dr. Brian Sullivan for their invaluable comments on this manuscript, and to my editor, Nancy Flight, for making sense out of it. To my parents for putting up with my live collections and wet clothes, and to my wife, Evelyn, for enthusiastically taking over this burden.

PAGES IV–V

The misnamed harlequin "frogs," genus Atelopus, *occur in Central and South America and are easily the most beautiful members of the toad family. Their bright colors may serve to warn predators of their highly toxic skin secretions.* ART WOLFE

Greystone Books
A division of Douglas & McIntyre Ltd.
2323 Quebec Street, Suite 201
Vancouver, British Columbia
V5T 4S7

Library of Congress Cataloging-in-Publication Data is available.

CANADIAN CATALOGUING IN PUBLICATION DATA

Parsons, Harry.
  The nature of frogs

  Includes bibliographic references and index.
  ISBN 1-55054-761-5

  1. Frogs. I. Title
QL668.E2P37 2000   597.8'9   C00-910332-5

Design by Val Speidel
Editing by Nancy Flight
Front jacket photograph by George Grall/NGS Image Collection
Back jacket photograph by Art Wolfe
Maps by Stuart Daniel
Illustrations by Nola Johnson
Printed and bound in Hong Kong by C & C Offset Printing Co., Ltd.

The publisher gratefully acknowledges the assistance of the Canada Council for the Arts and of the British Columbia Ministry of Tourism, Small Business and Culture. The publisher also acknowledges the financial support of the Government of Canada through the Book Publishing Industry Development Program (BPIDP) for its publishing activities.

The poem on page 93 originally appeared in *Rhymes and Runes of the Toad* (Macmillan, 1986) and is reprinted by permission of the author, Susan Fromberg Schaeffer.

CONTENTS

PREFACE

My love for frogs and their kin began a long time ago. These simple, beautiful creatures touch many people, especially children. I attribute this relationship to the fact that frogs and toads are small and easy to observe. They are not obviously dangerous. They are relatively easy for a child to catch. They have real faces that bespeak a level of consciousness. The first recognizable wild vertebrate that many youngsters can hold in their hands—the ultimate contact with another living creature—is a frog or toad. I have often observed with a smile a child staring at the frog in his or her hand. Open-mouthed and wide-eyed, the youngster stares at those other large eyes as if waiting for some word, some gesture, perhaps just a blink. Anything to say hello.

This book introduces the tailless amphibians of the world. Unavoidably, the word *frog* is sometimes used to mean a member of the family Ranidae and sometimes to mean any tailless amphibian. *Anurans* is also used to refer to tailless amphibians.

Some taxonomic names have to creep into any work about the natural world, and this is especially true for the thousands of frogs, many of which have no common name. For accuracy and brevity, the first time I use a common name for a specific species, it is followed by its binomial scientific name in italics and parentheses. Species referred to by their scientific name alone have no generally accepted common name. Scientific names follow those in general use by herpetologists in 1999.

Some of the theories or conclusions presented in this book are summaries of those developed by the leading herpetologists of the day. Others are the product of my own cynically enthusiastic ideas of what is going on out in ponds, swamps, marshes, lakes, forests, grasslands, deserts, mountains—and all of the other places that frogs call home.

FACING PAGE

A glass frog (Cochranella granulosa), *one of more than 120 species belonging to the New World family Centrolenidae. Most species are very small, rarely exceeding 30 millimeters (1.25 inches) in length, and live in the vegetation near mountain streams.*
MICHAEL FOGDEN/BRUCE COLEMAN INC.

CONSIDER THE FROG

Chapter One

> They may not sing as well or prettily as the birds, but the frogs did it first.
> —JAMES D. LAZELL, JR., *Reptiles & Amphibians in Massachusetts*

When I was 8 or 9, our family moved from a small town to a new development in the suburbs of a large city. The development was very new, for our backyard was still a mix of marsh and reedy fen when we moved in. I loved that backyard—it was my forest, my jungle, my wilderness—and I spent many days exploring and playing in it. I didn't know, of course, that within a year this natural wetland would be replaced by more row housing. The year that the marsh and I shared was probably responsible for my adult career as a naturalist and herpetologist. I know that my life changed over those few days when the fen, the fields, and all of the neighborhood's recently sodded front lawns were covered with thousands of tiny newly metamorphosed toads. They erupted from the marsh with the suddenness and vigor of angry bees from a hive. But they were not angry. They had somewhere to go, and they scrambled over lawn and pavement, my foot, and each other, with a single-mindedness that I learned much later was characteristic of their order. I held them. I kept them in jars for a few days at a time. I stared at individual toads for hours. I could not for the life of me understand how such a tiny, exquisite little creature could survive. I couldn't even

FACING PAGE

Solomon Island leaf frogs (Ceratobatrachus guenteri). *With a body shape and color that conceals them in the leaf litter, leaf frogs bear little resemblance to most other members of the "true frog" family, Ranidae. But the real mystery is how this species ever made it to the Solomon Islands.* ART WOLFE

understand how it could be alive; it seemed too small to have all the necessary organs. Those toads were a great puzzle for me. And they still are.

Of the more than 4500 amphibians alive today, over 4000 belong to the order Anura, which includes frogs and toads and other tailless amphibians; *anura* means "without tail." Sometimes they are referred to by their superorder, Salientia, which means "leaping," in reference to the powerful hind legs that many species in this order possess.

The best division of anurans into species or families is yet to come. Some taxonomists recognize up to twenty-seven families, others as few as twenty. Some families are huge. For example, members of the family Leptodactylidae are restricted to the New World—primarily South and Central America—and include approximately 900 species. This very diverse family includes some of the world's smallest and largest frogs as well as the unusual horned frog, genus *Ceratophrys*, a predator of small mammals and other creatures of the rain forest floor. In contrast, the primitive family Ascaphidae contains only one species, the tailed frogs (*Ascaphus truei*). Tailed frogs occur only in the Pacific Northwest of North America.

The terms *frog* and *toad* reveal our eurocentricity; the earliest taxonomists were European and shared their lives with only a small variety of amphibians. As other species appeared for the naming, people leaned heavily on the familiar. They named the tailless ones frog or toad after beasts they knew or gave them combined names that suggested that these creatures were some modification of the basic frog/toad design—*tree*frog, *spadefoot* toad, and so on—regardless of any real taxonomic relationships.

Anurans are more widely distributed and more abundant than the other amphibians—the salamanders and the wormlike caecilians. They occur on every continent except Antarctica and occupy niches ranging from rain forests and

FACING PAGE

The natural distribution of frog families is only one measure of evolutionary success; species diversity is also important. In northern Canada, for example, as many as three families may each be represented by only one species. In a comparable area near the equator, diversity may include eight or nine families and several hundred species. Note as well that the colored areas are a reflection of herpetological knowledge—they are most accurate in the temperate zone and least so in the tropics. Introduced species are not included on this map.

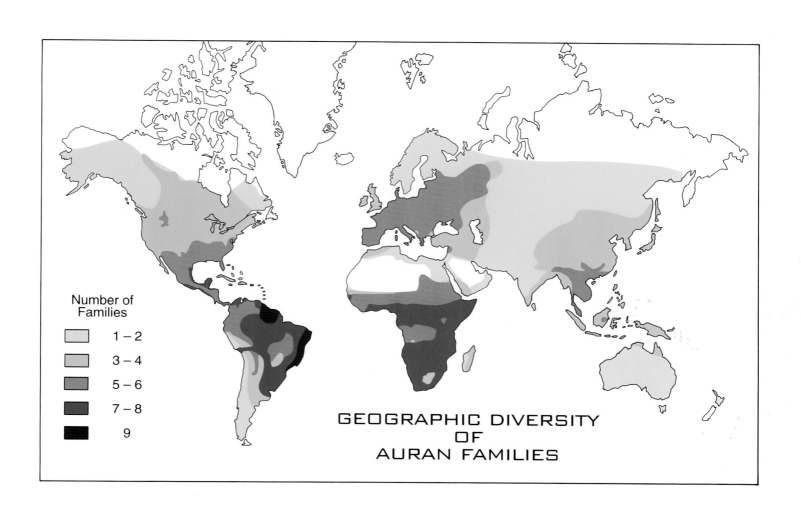

Number of Families

1 – 2
3 – 4
5 – 6
7 – 8
9

GEOGRAPHIC DIVERSITY
OF
AURAN FAMILIES

Puerto Rican coqui
(Eleutherodactylus
coqui). *The coqui is the*
most abundant frog in
Puerto Rico. It can be
found in densities of over
20,000 *individuals per*
*hectare (*8000 *per acre)*
and occupies habitats
ranging from the forest
floor to the canopy.
RAY PFORTNER/
PETER ARNOLD, INC.

wetlands to deserts and alpine areas. They are most abundant and diverse in wet tropical lowlands; their numbers and variety decrease with aridity and with distance south or north of the equator. There is a kind of symmetry to the distribution of families of anurans around the world: approximately one-third are restricted to the New World, another third occur only in the Old World, and the remaining third can be found in both.

INTRODUCING ANURANS

The earliest known clearly-a-frog fossil dates from the early Jurassic (230 MaBP), and by the late Jurassic, anurans of different species were found in Europe, North America, and South America. This is a significant event for understanding frog distribution and diversity, as there was no Europe, North America, or South America in the Lower Jurassic of 190 million years ago. Instead there was a huge landmass called Pangaea and a few separate blocks that would ultimately become eastern Asia. From the distribution of families of frogs, it seems likely that anurans went along for the ride as the breakup of the supercontinents and the subsequent wanderings of the new continents produced the configuration of the world that we are familiar with today. This process took over 220 million years, and the gradually increasing isolation of frog families spawned the incredible diversity that we see now and provides major clues to the origin and evolution of the different species.

We owe these amphibious pioneers our gratitude, for they mark one of the most important steps in vertebrate evolution—the move from sea to fresh water to land. Curiously, very few returned to the sea; there is only one saltwater frog, and fewer than a dozen can tolerate even brackish water.

Like all amphibians, frogs need moisture. They leave the water cautiously and most return to breed. Without moisture, their marvelous skin could not transfer

WE OWE THESE AMPHIBIOUS PIONEERS OUR GRATITUDE, FOR THEY MARK ONE OF THE MOST IMPORTANT STEPS IN VERTEBRATE EVOLUTION— THE MOVE FROM SEA TO FRESH WATER TO LAND.

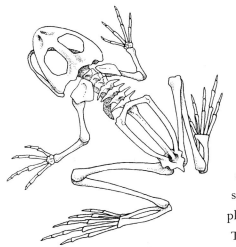

oxygen from both air and water. Frog eggs are particularly vulnerable to drying out, for they have no protective shell.

All anurans are superficially of a simple design: they have few vertebrae (five to ten), and the bones in their front legs and back legs are fused. In contrast, humans have thirty-three vertebrae, our lower arm bones are separated into radius and ulna, and our lower leg bones are separated into tibia and fibula. Two major bones in anuran ankles are also fused or partially fused. These features all seem to be adaptations to leaping and the stress that each landing will place on the skeleton.

The frog skull is a simple structure with virtually no neck, so almost all frogs must move their entire body to look in a different direction. In most species, nature has overcome this limitation by installing large, protruding eyes that provide almost 360-degree vision. Most species of frogs also have sharp eyesight, which helps guide their long tongues when they are capturing prey.

All anurans begin life as gilled, water-breathing organisms and metamorphose into lunged air breathers, although some pass through these stages in the egg. This metamorphosis may be the most remarkable characteristic of frogs; it is certainly the most studied. As polite adults, frogs breathe with their mouths closed. The up-and-down movement of their throats draws air in through the nostrils and forces it down into the lungs and then, with the aid of slight body contractions, expels the old air.

Perhaps the most amazing physical attribute of anurans is their skin. Although this soft, thin, Lycra-like surface may seem delicate, it performs many essential functions. All frogs breathe through their skin to some extent. The skin also controls the absorption and evaporation of water; in desert species, the skin retards water loss. It also protects the wearer from disease and injury and in some species,

INTO LUNGED AIR

BREATHERS,

ALTHOUGH SOME

PASS THROUGH

THESE STAGES IN

THE EGG.

FACING PAGE

The glass frog (genus
Cochranella) *is named for*
its skin, which is so
translucent that the
internal organs can be
seen. In some species,
even the heart can be
observed beating.
MICHAEL FOGDEN/
BRUCE COLEMAN INC.

by changing color, aids in temperature control. Many glands are located in the skin; some contain poisons for defense, and the presence of these toxins may be advertised by the skin color. In other species, the coloration helps them hide or confuses predators when they flee. All frogs shed their skin at regular intervals, ranging from a few days to several weeks. When they shed, most eat their discarded skin. This ultimate form of recycling provides them with moisture and nutrients.

Another tool that helps anurans deal with their environment is the pineal body (sometimes called the pineal complex), which, in some species, can be detected externally as a tiny, almost white spot between some frogs' eyes. Its role is related to light detection, and it may help the frog in many ways: by stimulating the skin to darken for better heating when there is little light, by providing orientation to the sun and thus helping to guide their movements, by detecting the changes in seasons, and by stimulating the production of hormones that are needed at certain times of the year. I sometimes wonder whether this complex is the toadstone of vaunted powers referred to in European medical writings, especially during the fifteenth and sixteenth centuries—Shakespeare's precious jewel in a toad's head. But this notion probably gives too much credit to anatomists of that time. It seems more likely that the "jewel" was the toad's powerful toxin-producing paratoid gland or perhaps its iridescent, light-reflecting eyes.

Other, less obvious features contribute to anuran success. Frogs are ectotherms, meaning that they obtain their body heat from external sources. In contrast, humans are endotherms, with an internal furnace that must be fueled daily to maintain a body temperature of around 37°C (98.6°F). Ectotherms are often called cold-blooded, but this term is a misnomer. Since their body temperature comes directly from the sun or from proximity to a heat source, on warm days ectotherms are warm. Moreover, *cold-blooded* is a pejorative term implying cruelty and malevolence. I suspect that the anuran brain, like many ectotherm brains, does not contain room for these higher functions; frogs seem capable only of simple responses to a relatively narrow range of stimuli.

Because frogs cannot control their temperature internally, they do so behaviorally. During their active periods of the year—usually the wet season in the tropics and the warm season in temperate areas—frogs select areas that provide enough heat but not too much. A move to the shade significantly reduces their temperature, as does a move into the water. This temperature control is critical because frogs that are too hot will die and frogs that are too cold will be unable to flee from danger or catch their prey.

Anurans living in the temperate zone experience at least a few months every year when no source of heat is adequate to meet their needs. So they skip this season by hibernating. During hibernation, which may take place on the wet litter at the bottom of ponds and lakes (affectionately referred to by some herpetologists as loon shit), they are very close to death. The most amazing example is the wood frog (*Rana sylvatica*), which ranges from the northern United States to north of the Arctic Circle in Canada. Wood frogs, and some other northern anurans, produce their own "antifreeze" by converting their liver glycogen to glucose. When appropriately winterized, wood frogs can tolerate freezing of their body fluids, which produces a stiff body with no breathing or heartbeat—to most observers, a dead frog worthy of a John Cleese rant. If freezing ruptures cells and ice forms around their organs, wood frogs die. But they seem to regularly undergo these near-death experiences and survive to croak another day. During hibernation, a frog's energy reserves remain largely intact for use during the spring to come. In comparison, a bird that does not migrate, or a mammal that does not migrate or hibernate, must struggle to avoid freezing while hunting for energy (in the form of food) to fuel its furnace at the most difficult time of year to do so.

FACING PAGE

The wood frog (Rana sylvatica) *is appropriately named, for the northern limits of its range in Canada coincide with the most northerly range of trees. Wood frogs are the only North American amphibian to live north of the Arctic Circle.*
ROBERT McCAW

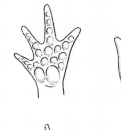

A water-holding frog
(Cyclorana novaehollan-
diae) *from arid Australia.*
In drought conditions, this
frog's dead skin separates
from the new skin but is
not shed. Instead, it
hardens into a protective
outer cover that reduces
water loss by a factor of
more than ten.
MICHAEL H. FRANCIS

Although frogs live in deserts and other dry areas, desiccation, especially when combined with high temperatures, is a major threat to the adults, their tadpoles, and their eggs. The first responses of adults and juveniles are behavioral: they find water, they reduce evaporation rates by closing their eyes and tucking in their legs to minimize vulnerable surface area, and some species cluster together with others of the same species to further reduce evaporation by decreasing exposed surface area. Physiological flexibility helps too; frogs can store water in their bladders, for example.

But these techniques may not be adequate when drought occurs. Anurans then enter estivation, the dry season equivalent of hibernation. Many desert anurans burrow to escape drying out. Some species, like Australia's water-holding frog (*Cyclorana platycephala*), develop an anuran wet suit, which may be a "cocoon" of dead skin that is not shed or hardened mucus. This protective layer retards evaporation, while internally the body minimizes its use of moisture and can even produce new water metabolically. Once again, the frog enters a dormant state to wait out the unacceptable conditions. Like hibernation, estivation may last for many months.

Anuran techniques for dealing with the environment have been fine-tuned over millions of years. Most species take what could be described as the easy route. They live where high temperatures are the norm and where rain, humidity, and surface water provide lots of moisture. For this reason, the tropical rain forests of South America, Africa, Asia, and the Indo-Pacific host a considerable majority of frog species. So why would frogs choose, in an evolutionary sense, to scratch out a living in the harsh environments of desert and tundra? Or did environmental conditions change and some species managed to survive?

Writers often describe how *difficult* conditions are for an animal that must live in the *frozen* north or the *harsh* desert. But these are the wrong terms. It is neither

FROG & TOAD FEET

Upper left: *Many toads are*
terrestrial; the horny tubercles
on their feet reduce abrasions.
Upper right: *The leathery*
"spade" on a spadefoot's
(family Pelobatidae) hind feet
help its backwards burrowing.
Lower left: *Extensive*
webbing on the hind feet of
many species of the genus
Rana *makes them strong*
swimmers.
Lower right: *The long toes*
and adhesive pads of treefrogs
(genus Hyla*) aid their*
climbing. NOLA JOHNSTON

too difficult nor too easy for a wood frog to survive in the Mackenzie River delta north of the Arctic Circle or for a spadefoot toad to survive in the Sonoran Desert. It is exactly right. It is the very conditions that exist in these areas that created wood frogs and spadefoots or provided an environment that matched their adaptations. And the tradeoffs are, in a metaphorical sense, exactly the same as those a person might make when choosing between a home in a small town and a home in a big city. The small town resident, like the northern frog, has fewer opportunities but less competition. The big city dweller has many more choices for employment coupled with many more people competing for the same job. Wood frogs and spadefoots exploit niches where food is seasonally plentiful and competition and predators are relatively few but where the environment is fickle. Tropical anurans deal with the opposite situation. The climate attracts many competing species, and wherever frogs are abundant, so are the many creatures that eat them.

SLIM-WAISTED, LONG-LEGGED FROGS

Throughout much of the world, the most familiar frogs, also known as true frogs, belong to the family Ranidae. Stebbins's *Field Guide to Western Reptiles and Amphibians* offers a succinct description of the largest genus, *Rana*: frogs of this genus are "typically slim-waisted, long-legged, smooth-skinned jumpers with webbed hind feet."

Most laypersons, when asked what a frog is, will provide a pretty accurate description of a member of this genus. Words and phrases normally include "big legs," "great jumper," "lives in the water," and "catches insects." All of these characteristics define true frogs, one of the most familiar wild animals in much of the world. The family Ranidae includes seven hundred species; dominates the frog world in North America, Europe, and Asia; and is well represented in Africa.

For a number of reasons, the leopard frog, genus *Rana*, may be the most familiar frog in North America. Several species share this name throughout central and eastern North America, where they may be called leopard frogs after their spots or meadow frogs after their habitat. The first sign of them is usually the *plop* as they leap from shoreline into water, or a series of muffled *plops* as they leap hurriedly through the sedges and grasses of wet meadows. As generations of children can attest, leopard frogs can move great distances quickly when alarmed, and their cryptic coloration makes them surprisingly difficult to spot even when you have seen exactly where they landed. But not difficult enough, for leopard frogs are perhaps equally well known for their regular appearance on dissecting trays in high school and university biology classes, where they have taught millions of students the basics of vertebrate anatomy.

The bullfrog (*Rana catesbeiana*) is equally recognizable to most people because of its large size, up to 20 centimeters (8 inches), and its deep, sonorous call that is commonly described as *jug o'rum*. The bullfrog is common in many permanent bodies of water in eastern North America and has been introduced to many places in the West. These introductions probably stemmed from the bullfrog's commercial potential; with its large legs, it is the best North American frog to harvest for frogs' legs.

The southeastern portion of the United States, with its many bayous, swamps, marshes, and other wetlands, has the greatest diversity in North America of medium- to large-sized true frogs, including, in addition to bullfrogs, carpenter frogs (*Rana virgatipes*), Florida leopard frogs (*Rana sphenocephala*), river frogs (*Rana heckscheri*), pig frogs (*Rana grylio*), green frogs (*Rana clamitans*), and crawfish frogs (*Rana areolata*). In contrast, the only ranid frog species present in much of northern Canada is the cold-tolerant wood frog.

The common or grass frog (*Rana temporaria*) is found throughout Europe and

FACING PAGE

Florida leopard frogs
(Rana sphenocephala)
are the most abundant
frogs in Florida and one of
very few anurans that can
tolerate brackish water.
They become browner
when away from water for
extended periods.

STEPHEN KIRKPATRICK

ALTHOUGH ANURANS ARE NOT

GENERALLY REGARDED AS THE

RHODES SCHOLARS OF THE

VERTEBRATE

WORLD, AT LEAST

ONE AUTHOR HAS

SUGGESTED THAT

TOADS ARE SIGNIF-

ICANTLY BRIGHTER

THAN FROGS.

toads' ability to solve a simple maze more quickly, their tendency to avoid jumping off high tables, and—this is my favorite—their discovery "after eight or nine trials" that a glass barrier cannot be passed through. Apparently, frogs don't ever learn this lesson.

Within the Bufonidae family, the common toad (*Bufo bufo*) probably has the greatest range of any anuran species, from the highlands of Scotland and the coast of Portugal to northwestern Africa and all across Europe and southern Asia. Because of its vast range and the large populations of humans it shares its life with, the common toad may be the best-known toad in the world and has set the standard for what a toad should look like: squat, heavy bodied, and covered in warts, with two prominent and nasty-looking glands just aft of its head and a look in the eyes that would silence a sailor. The common toad—or Crapaud or Sapo Común or Erdkröte or Kurbaga or a hundred other names—is also magnificently typical of many of the family Bufonidae. It can wander far from water as a result of its tough, leathery skin and its ability to absorb moisture from the earth through a most unusual means. The toad's "seat patch" is a section of thin, moisture-absorbing skin that covers the portion of its body most often in touch with the ground.

Common toads frequently venture into areas of human habitation and may often be found in the garden, where the tilled soil provides easy digging and the variety of plants and artificial lights attract insect meals. As befits their rotund shape and their dignity, these toads appear to prefer to walk but will hop if necessary. They may live as long as forty years, so there could be a few individual toads out there who can compare their memories of the turbulent sixties as they proceed into the new millennium.

There is no transcontinental toad in the New World on the scale of the common toad, but twenty-one species of *Bufo* are found in the United States and

Canada alone. The Bufonidae family in North America does offer an excellent lesson in zoogeography—the distribution of animals—for it would not be facetious to suggest that six of these species have divided up the continent among themselves, with the rest having to make do with the little that is left over. In much of North America, only one species of toad is present. Which species this is depends on the landscape. In the mountainous western portion of the continent, it is the western toad (*Bufo boreas*). From the Great Plains south to the deserts, the Great Plains toad (*Bufo cognatus*) rules. To the north, the Canadian toad (*Bufo hemiophrys*) is alone in occupying the short-grass prairie and the boreal forest as far north as the 60th parallel. The American toad (*Bufo americanus*) is the familiar resident of the mixed forests of the northeastern United States and eastern Canada, while the southern toad (*Bufo terrestris*) is at home along the coastal plain of the southeastern states. Only one species, Woodhouse's toad (*Bufo woodhousii*), overlaps the ranges of a number of the other species. For the rest of these species, their range maps complement one another as if the boundaries were the result of careful negotiation. They are really the result of natural selection, for these toads look remarkably similar and are assumed to have evolved from a single prototypic toad. They are of similar size—typically 7 to 10 centimeters (3 to 4 inches) long—and have the classic plump toad body with green to brown mottled coloration and abundant warts. Most are primarily nocturnal.

This evolutionary "idea" of a toad—stout, tough-skinned, drought-resistant, with poison instead of speed for defense—has proven to be a successful design. There are well over three hundred species throughout the world, including, for trivia buffs, the only two species of amphibian in the United Arab Emirates.

Consider *Bufo regularis*, sometimes called the square-marked toad, which ranges from the Nile delta south through most of Africa. Like many of its

FACING PAGE

Virtually no area in the United States is toad-free. This map shows only the most widely distributed species. Species that have less expansive ranges occupy portions of the same areas as well as habitats left unexploited by the Big Six.

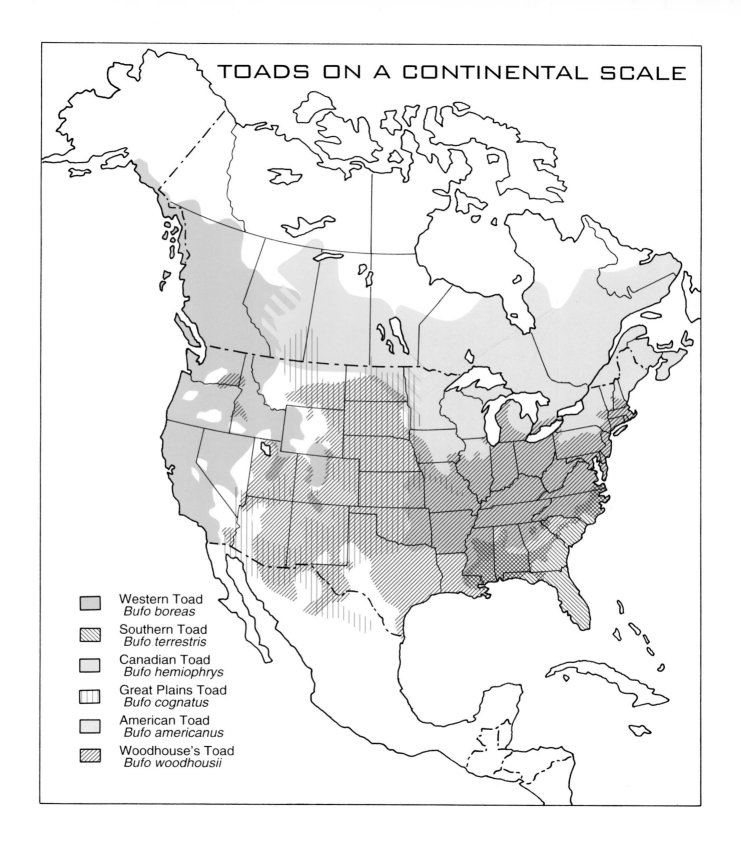

TOADS ON A CONTINENTAL SCALE

Western Toad
Bufo boreas

Southern Toad
Bufo terrestris

Canadian Toad
Bufo hemiophrys

Great Plains Toad
Bufo cognatus

American Toad
Bufo americanus

Woodhouse's Toad
Bufo woodhousii

relatives, this species occupies many diverse habitats, often some distance from water, and is a familiar sight around human dwellings.

Toads are commonly the species that fills the ecological job for a squat, poisonous insect eater who has flexible housing requirements and doesn't mind people. Given anuran diversity, it is little wonder that species of other frog families are sometimes drawn to this niche.

An appropriate example of this evolutionary flexibility comes from Australia, a continent full of creatures doing what in the rest of world is someone else's job. Over the millennia, kangaroos, wallabies, and opossums have assumed the roles that elsewhere are done by a host of other mammals: deer, antelope, squirrels, weasels, rabbits, and so on. Australia is also home of *Uperoleia*, a genus of small, short-legged frogs that have granular skin and secrete toxins when disturbed. These members of the Australian family Myobatrachidae are so small and secretive that most of the twenty-some species in this genus have only been discovered since 1980, and it is probable that most Australians are unaware of their existence. In the absence of an alternative, I suggest the name wannabe toads for this fascinating genus. It even sounds Australian.

THE DIVERSITY OF ANURANS

Other families of anurans are as successful as the true frogs and toads. More than seven hundred species of treefrogs belong to the family Hylidae, which includes some of the most beautiful frogs with some of the most distinctive songs. The green treefrog (*Hyla cinerea*) of the southeastern United States is sometimes called the bell frog after its resonating call. Like other treefrogs, it has toepads that aid in climbing smooth surfaces, including window glass. The common treefrog (*Hyla arborea*) of Europe shares some of these features, as do many other treefrogs, but the family also includes the many exceptions that are the rule in

FACING PAGE
Green treefrogs (Hyla cinerea), *among the prettiest and best-known of eastern North American treefrogs, are often drawn to backyard lights in search of insects. Note the long digits with adhesive toepads for climbing. Their mating call has been described as "pealing cowbells" and as an unmusical quonk.*
CHRIS MATTISON

nature. In Australia, a number of family members have opted for the niche that would normally be occupied by true frogs. Many species of the genus *Litoria* have reduced toepads and other body modifications that better suit their *Rana*-like aquatic habitats.

The success of anurans in distribution and abundance throughout the world is based on their simple design of squat body, long hind legs, and short front legs. But within this working design is a rich diversity of form and lifestyle. Frogs range in size from the tiny gold frog (*Psyllophryne didactyla*) of Brazil, which is less than 1 centimeter (0.4 inch) long, to the Goliath frog of Africa (*Conraua goliath*), which can be over 30 centimeters (12 inches) in body length and weigh over 3 kilograms (6.6 pounds). There is the hairy frog (*Trichobatrachus robustus*) of Cameroon, whose "hairs" are actually structures that may aid breathing through the skin when the frog is under water, and the sandhill frog, *Arenophryne rotunda*, of Australia, which breaks all the rules by living in sand dunes—an unlikely place to encounter a frog. There are frogs with claws on their feet who almost never leave the water (Pipidae), frogs with spades on their legs for digging (Pelobatidae) who may only see water a few times a year, short-faced alien-looking turtle frogs (*Myobatrachus gouldii*) of western Australia that appear incapable of any sort of movement (but do burrow), and the Borneo flying frogs, which leap from high places using their large webbed feet for steering and for cushioning the landing after a controlled glide.

The diversity of anurans also includes some of the most exquisitely beautiful creatures. The poison dart frogs (family Dendrobatidae) of Central and South America have vivid, enamel-like colors that rival or surpass the most splendid plumage of the birds. Many of the tropical treefrogs feature highly contrasting colors in leg, body, and eye that seem too ornate to be natural. My favorite is the wonderfully named corroboree toadlet (*Pseudophryne corroboree*), which lives in the subalpine woodlands and sphagnum bogs of New South Wales. Its shiny black base color is highlighted by stripes and bars of vivid yellow, which make the toadlet look too detailed and precise to possibly be real.

The abundance, diversity, beauty, fascinating life histories, and almost global distribution of anurans have been a source of curiosity and amazement for people for centuries. It is no wonder that they have played a large part in the human imagination.

Chapter Two
KERMIT AND THE DEVIL

These foul and loathsome animals are abhorrent because of their cold body, pale color, cartilaginous skeleton, filthy skin, fierce aspect, calculating eye, offensive smell, harsh voice, squalid habitation, and terrible venom; and so their Creator has not exerted his powers to make many of them.

—CAROLUS LINNAEUS, *Systema Naturae*

It's not easy being green.

—KERMIT THE FROG, in *The Muppet Movie*

Throughout history, humans have seen frogs in both a positive and a negative light. This does not imply a balance; one view or the other usually dominated, sometimes for centuries. At one end of a spectrum are the somewhat churlish comments of Carolus Linnaeus (aka Carl von Linné), the Swedish scientist and father of taxonomy—the classification of organisms. He might have named them but he didn't have to like them. Today frogs have joined a select group of taxa with charisma. The group also includes penguins, bears, and dolphins, to name just a few of these iconic animals. A cartoon frog is now the symbol of Warner Brothers. Frogs sell beer and cellular phones. They are officially cute. People collect images and models of frogs and seem to find a reason to smile by just looking at them.

THE SYMBOLIC FROG

Good or bad, frogs have always occupied a special place in human experience. Because their amorous activities are often obvious, energetic, and noisy, and the product is hundreds or thousands of offspring, frogs have been associated with sex

FACING PAGE

Reinwardt's flying frog (Rhacophorus reinwardtii). *Some herpetoculturists call this species the Asian blue-webbed gliding treefrog. Both names refer to its ability to escape predators by gliding on the extended webbing of its toes and on its posterior skin flap from the forest canopy to the forest floor.* CHRIS MATTISON

SINCE FROGS ARE

ALSO MOST ACTIVE

AND VISIBLE IN THE

WET SEASONS OR

EVEN DURING

OCCASIONAL

RAINS, SOME

GROUPS HAVE

BELIEVED THAT

FROGS BRING THE

RAIN AND HAVE

BLAMED THEM FOR

WITHHOLDING IT IN

TIMES OF DROUGHT.

and fecundity for centuries. Along the Nile, where enormous numbers of breeding frogs appeared during the annual flooding of the river, frog amulets were worn to enhance fertility. In Egypt, the hieroglyphic for the number 100,000 is a tadpole. The ancient Egyptian goddess of childbirth, Heket, sometimes appears as a frog, other times as a human with a frog's head. And a sacred knife marked with a frog emblem was laid on the stomach of a pregnant woman as protection.

The miracle of egg to tadpole to frog has made frogs a symbol of change, or metamorphosis, as well. If the frog could change itself, then just maybe it could, with enticements and observation of the proper rituals, do the same for people. This idea has been expressed in a cross-cultural array of "frog to prince" stories. The best-known transformation story is probably *The Frog King* by the Brothers Grimm. In this tale, a beautiful princess rescues a frog trapped in a well. Against her will, the frog follows the princess home. In anger she flings the frog against a wall—rather than kissing it as the more familiar variations suggest—whereupon the frog turns into a handsome young prince.

In another metamorphosis story from New York State, a beautiful (as always) young girl saves her father's life by going to live with the headless villain who has placed a curse upon him. Once there, she finds herself served and attended to by a giant toad. While spying on the toad, she sees him remove his skin, revealing a handsome young man. The girl destroys the skin, which ends the curse, leading inevitably to marriage.

Since frogs are also most active and visible in the wet seasons or even during occasional rains, some groups have believed that frogs bring the rain and have blamed them for withholding it in times of drought. Some Native groups in the Orinoco basin of South America, for example, considered anurans to be the lords of the waters and would keep frogs under a pot and beat them with rods when there was a drought. During prolonged droughts, the Aymar people of the Lake

FACING PAGE
A Tlingit shaman's mask from the west coast of Canada. The frogs are probably based on the Pacific chorus frog (Pseudacris regilla).
STEPHEN S. MEYERS/ COURTESY DEPARTMENT OF LIBRARY SERVICES, AMERICAN MUSEUM OF NATURAL HISTORY, #3821 (2)

No wonder that frogs invade human culture. The ornate colors of this painted mantella (Mantella baroni) in Madagascar, combined with its powerful skin toxins, are almost certain to attract attention.

ART WOLFE

Titicaca area would place basins full of frogs, water, and plants in direct sunlight. As the water evaporated, the distressed frogs would cry out and the spirits would send rain. At least that was the theory.

The Neuwars of Nepal performed an elaborate ceremony each October involving five separate offerings and prayers for rain and generous crops. In Korea, the croak of the frog when it rains is said to be the guilt-ridden lament of a frog who fears that his mother's grave may be washed away by the rising waters. In Vietnam, the frog is regarded as the "uncle of the god of the sky," and a traditional belief holds that anyone who attacks a toad will be struck by lightning. In both Australia and New Zealand, many indigenous people would not kill frogs for fear of unleashing a flood. But practical concerns can overcome these taboos; in Australia, frogs were also dug up in times of drought for the water they hold.

The Aztecs and Mayans were obsessed with time and its measurement, and frogs were often an element or icon in their calendars, perhaps reflecting their association with wet seasons and with spring. Both the Mayan and the early Chinese cultures associated anurans with the moon; in some Mayan lunar texts, the face of a frog is used as a moon symbol, while the toad Chang E is goddess of the moon.

The Assiniboine—aboriginal people of the North American plains—incorporated a frog into their creation mythology: it is Frog who debates the appropriate length of winter with Muskrat. In another North American aboriginal myth—unattributed to a specific group and, I suspect, at least partly the product of modern embellishment—a committee of animals holds a long debate about the proper length of a day and a night. Grizzly lobbies hard for six months of day and six months of night. Frog surveys the other animals and recommends the day length we know today. The vote supports him, and Eagle informs Brother Sun of the decision. You can still hear frogs celebrating their success as they croak, "One day, one night. One day, one night. One day, one night."

Frogs also play a role in Australian creation mythology. According to one aboriginal story, a woman hides from her husband under a rock and turns into a frog while the husband climbs a tree and becomes a marsupial.

Many coastal tribes in North America's Pacific Northwest incorporated frogs into their spectacular totem poles and told stories about them. In the Tlingit First Nation, a number of stories focus on human females who married frogs, sometimes producing children. Frog was also responsible, at the beginning of the world, for showing Raven, who in turn told the people, how to use the resources of the sea. Two large frogs guarded the celestial kingdom of the Thunderbird for the Haida of British Columbia's Queen Charlotte Islands. Their loud croaks announced the arrival of strangers and alerted travellers along these often dangerous fogbound coasts.

Some frog roles are of unclear origin. In Nagaland in northeast India, a frog helps a young man become wealthy and respected. In the Himalayas, a clever frog helps a deer escape a tiger by pretending to eat tigers itself. In Japan, the legendary demon-toad O Gawa was a monster that ate snakes and could destroy large areas by spitting poison.

POISONS AND POTIONS

On the dark side, the toxic nature of toads must have been known early in the shared history of humans and anurans. This poison, combined with what many people find to be a less than attractive appearance, produced a number of cultural responses. In some eras and areas, toads were considered powerful; in others, they were thought to be evil and conspiring. Many groups felt a combination of respect and fear toward toads. And some responses simply don't have a clear and logical explanation.

Toad poisoning seems to have been very popular. In Rome in the second

century AD, the poet Juvenal stated that wives sometimes disposed of their husbands with toad-based poison. Some Roman writers describe toads that could kill with a belch or were even dangerous to look at, although no species were identified. Two bishops in the fourteenth century were accused of poisoning that involved toads. One (who was imprisoned but later freed) was said to have murdered the wife of the French king, while the other had attempted to assassinate Pope John XXII. He confessed under torture and was burned at the stake. In Boccacio's *Decameron*, toad poisoning accidentally kills two lovers. In England, toad poison is believed to have been used to kill the unpopular King John. And during a witch trial, it came out that a toad-based assassination attempt had been planned, but never made, on James I of Scotland. The court of the day accepted without question the notion that a person could die from simple contact with toad poison. Curiously, deaths from toad poisoning have plummeted to zero in the last century or two.

Frogs and toads also played a role in early medicine. Unfortunately, almost all uses involved the dismemberment of the animal. Right eye bothering you? Hang a frog's right eye around your neck. Plucked eyebrows keep growing back? Impale fifteen frogs on bulrushes. Suffering from gout? Wrap a dismembered toad around the problem foot. Worried about the recent outbreak of the Black Death (and who wouldn't be)? Hang a toad or its legs or its ashes around your neck. The plague must have been a most unpleasant time both because of the disease itself and because of the grotesque—and doubtlessly aromatic—"cures."

Toads have also been drunk, perhaps to acquire their essence. Pulverized toad was said to cure kidney stones. Powdered toad was also considered useful in treating nosebleeds and dropsy. The Mayans used toad ash for similar reasons. In rural nineteenth-century England, the "toad doctor" would travel around with his bags of toads offering treatment for a variety of problems.

The Middle Ages, and even the early Renaissance, were bad times for many animals. Christianity in its most literal and all-pervasive form was at its zenith, but it had incorporated some of the animistic spiritualism of pagan days. Animals were often seen as conscious, thinking creatures, but in most cases their thoughts, actions, and very nature were perceived as the work of the devil. In France, toads were sometimes called Bot, another name for Satan. In *Paradise Lost*, John Milton depicted Satan tempting Eve to eat that famous apple by disguising himself as a toad and poisoning her. Witches and toads were linked as conspirators or as the devil's assistant and her potions. Toads were often cited in witchcraft trials, sometimes as devils in animal form, sometimes as the ingredients for poisons or spells, and occasionally by their very presence nearby, as evidence of an evil character.

In the Caribbean, zombies, the walking dead, were believed to be the products of elaborate potions, including the poisonous secretions of the large marine toad (*Bufo marinus*). Laboratory testing on chimpanzees has established that a comatose state can result from simply rubbing the potion on the animal's abdomen, but the prime ingredient was a potent nerve poison, tetradotoxin, that is obtained from puffer fish.

A related practice occasionally makes the news today. Toad-sucking is the practice of drinking, inhaling, smoking, or otherwise exposing oneself directly to the skin secretions of a toad. These secretions contain several powerful toxins that can have a profound effect on heart muscles, among other body parts. The toxins of some toads will kill dogs that bite them and are quite capable of periodically doing the same for people. One author, ever in the pursuit of knowledge, inhaled toad poison as one would take snuff. His experience can be described in a few selected phrases from his diligently detailed notes:

"nostril anesthetized"

"roots of teeth anesthetized"

"sneezing . . . profuse sweating"

"hallucinogenic symptoms: moving hand . . . leaves . . . trailed image"

"fleeting pain in temples"

"salivating strongly"

"spasmodic burning of interior of nostrils"

So some perceived uses for anurans have not altogether disappeared. But most have, at least in the Western world. Toad poisonings are way down; the toad doctor no longer makes regular visits to our area or even to health food stores. Witchcraft trials seem to have fallen out of favor.

FROG CULTURE TODAY

The frog fables of Aesop and Grimm, Kenneth Grahame's *Wind in the Willows*, and Mark Twain's jumping frog stories have given way to a host of books featuring frogs in a role that children seem to accept without hesitation, as ambassadors for animals and their environment. In this regard, and this regard only, it is a friendlier world for anurans after centuries of persecution and suspicion.

Frogs are still important to humans. In many parts of the world, they are food. They are a favorite subject for teaching and research because their egg masses can be easily manipulated morphologically and biogenetically. For the same reason they are often used in toxicology studies. Some, like the African clawed frogs, have been the material for pregnancy tests and have even traveled in space. Frog skin secretions contain a host of unique chemicals for the pharmacologist. Frogs are a naturalist's favorite object for study, particularly for young naturalists. They play an important role in the ecosystems they inhabit as a result of their abundance, their diversity, and the energy they efficiently store for use by those higher up the food chain. And they are a beautiful and wonderful thing all to themselves.

A FROG HE DID

Chapter Three

A-WOOING GO

If it is not small enough to eat nor large enough to eat you, and does not put up a squawk about it, mate with it.

—DAVID L. JAMESON, *Systematic Zoology*

THE JOURNEY TO THE BREEDING PONDS

Frogs are small and sometimes have to travel great distances to their breeding ponds. Many species bypass the ponds with fish in them, for frogs that try to breed in fish-filled waters don't last long. They will tolerate fish if they have plenty of aquatic vegetation to hide in, but first choice is a fish-free zone. They may be returning to the ponds where they transformed from tadpoles, or they may be drawn by the voices of others who are calling. They may have to cross busy roads with predictable results. They have little choice; the route for their journey was selected millennia ago.

The problem is frog fidelity—not to their mates but to their breeding sites, to which they return year after year. The longest migrations are recorded in Eastern Europe, where some water frogs travel as far as 15 kilometers (9 miles). It is difficult to change such deeply programmed directions; common toads have returned to ponds for several years after they were drained or converted to parking lots. But not all anurans are that inflexible; female natterjack toads (*Bufo calamita*)

FACING PAGE

First comes the waiting. Male common frogs (Rana temporaria) *gather at a breeding pond in anticipation of the arrival of the females. Not all will get to breed as the males sing and scuffle to attract a mate. But for now they seem to patiently check out the competition.*

JIM HALLETT/BBC NATURAL HISTORY UNIT

This male gray treefrog
(either Hyla versicolor *or*
Hyla chrysoscelis*) is*
calling to attract a female.
The two species are
indistinguishable by eye
but have distinctive songs,
which is more than
enough information for the
females. ADAM JONES

have been observed using pools several kilometers apart in different years. Some desert anurans will visit different locations in a single breeding season.

Many species move when the rains begin or just before in response to changes in air pressure that signal the rain to come. Depending on where they live, the trigger could be the start of the tropical rainy season, the spring showers and melting snow of the temperate zone, or the desert's summer thunderstorms. A few species may already be at the pond, having spent the winter in the saturated muck at the bottom.

The males normally arrive first and set about establishing territories in the shallow water. The females wait patiently for the great courtship ritual to begin, a ritual that but for scale rivals those anywhere in the animal kingdom. Let the songs begin.

LOVE SONGS

It can be difficult to describe anuran songs. Following are a few attempts at descriptions drawn from field guides around the world:

Long, musical trill	American toad
Quiet, rolling laugh	painted frog
Uk-uk-uk-uk	spotted grass frog
A creaking door	northern leopard frog
Bre-ke-ke-ke-ke-ke-kek	pool frog
Squelch	eastern froglet
Twang like a loose banjo string	green frog
Sound of a pneumatic drill	Peron's treefrog
C'lock-c'lock-c'lock	common spadefoot
qwark-qwark-qwark	common toad
Bleat like an unhappy sheep	Couch's spadefoot
Nasal *quonk quonk quonk*	Pine Barrens treefrog

MALES NEAR ONE

ANOTHER COM-

MONLY CALL IN

DUETS, TRIOS, OR

OTHER SMALL

GROUPS.

To the uninitiated, this cacophony might seem to be produced by some unmusical chorus of aliens. Even herpetologists find the word "din" an appropriate descriptor on busy nights. In simplest terms, it is a grand assemblage of males shouting, "Pick me!"

Each version of "Pick me!" is the product of a frog's vocal cords, greatly augmented by the air sacs in its throat. When the sacs expand with air, they broadcast the sound, making the calls of some species audible kilometers away. By forcing air into the sacs from the lungs and then from the sacs back into the lungs, frogs use their sacs like bagpipes, allowing them to call continuously, even under water. A few species that lack vocal sacs call, but usually their calls are only audible a few meters away.

Male vocalizations provide listening frogs of both sexes with important information about the size and health of the caller. There may be even more information exchanged; North American bullfrogs can identify specific individuals by their calls. For the males, knowledge about their rivals reduces the use of energy that might otherwise be spent fighting. For females, knowledge gleaned from their suitors' calls offers the best hope for a successful breeding season by providing information about the individual male and, possibly, about the quality of the egg deposition site he is guarding.

Males near one another commonly call in duets, trios, or other small groups. It may be the dominant male of the group who calls first, followed at brief intervals (sometimes fractions of a second) by the males in the chorus. This careful temporal spacing allows each member of the chorus to get his message out without being drowned out by the others. The background songs of the many other choruses take on the quality of Muzak.

I have spent many wet, cold nights standing motionless in the dark, with my flashlight at the ready, waiting for *my* trio of singers, who have fallen silent at my

FACING PAGE

A reed frog of the Hyperoliidae family. The many species of these small frogs of African wetlands display a bewildering range of colors and markings. It may be easier for frogs to recognize their own species by call rather than sight because their ears are tuned to their own species' frequency.

DENNIS SHERIDAN

WILDLIFE

PHOTOGRAPHY

FACING PAGE

Named for its call, the
coqui belongs to the largest
genus of vertebrates
known to science; this
Eleutherodactylus coqui
is one of more than four
hundred species. Coqui
larvae complete their
development to adulthood
in the egg, which is
diligently tended by males.

KEVIN SCHAFER

approach, to begin again. Finally, there will be a single tentative peep. Then—if there are no bad consequences—a repeated *peep*. This one will be followed by an answering *peep*, and the two singers appear to duel until the third timid singer peeps. This last frog is usually the one nearest me, for whom I have been waiting the longest to catch in the light beam.

There's a lot of other action in the sordid, soggy environment of an anuran breeding pond. Other males are present but do not call. These satellite males hang out near the calling males—at a discreet distance—hoping to intercept females on the way to their choice. Or they may call themselves when the dominant male is busy with a female, or call in unison to interfere with his endearments. And even the strong must rest at times; dominant males sometimes take time off from calling.

Not all calls mean "Pick me!" Males often have a second, aggressive call that they direct at other males who have come too close and are encroaching on their territory. The tiny Puerto Rican coqui is named for its two-part call. The *co* is directed at other males and is a threat. The *qui* part attracts females. If another male approaches, the caller drops the *qui*, leaving a one-part call of intimidation. Other frogs include proposition and threat as one inseparable message, while still others have another call that is reserved for threatening intruding males. For example, leopard frogs use a short, rapid chuckle to do this.

Although females usually silently evaluate their prospective mates, a number of female frogs in different parts of the world also give aggressive calls. In one North American species, the carpenter frog (*Rana virgatipes*), females mimic the male aggressive call as part of mate selection. A female calls as she approaches a dominant male, who, if sufficiently irritated, will wrestle with her as males do. The wrestling ultimately develops into mating, or as it is correctly called, amplexus. This unusual strategy may help the female carpenter frog ensure that her mate really is the macho male she wants as well as deter any satellite males with big ideas.

There are variations of course. Not all males establish territories; male wood frogs simply mass in the ponds and grab any female that joins them. Some amplexed pairs of wood frogs arrive at the ponds already mated.

In the tropics, allowance must be made for competition by many more anuran species. In South America, there may be upward of seventy species of anurans living within a few square kilometers of each other. If all of them were to call at the same time, their individual calls would be indistinguishable. For this reason, calling in the tropics is spread out over a much longer period than in the temperate world as different species call at different times. In tropical areas that have rain all year, there is some anuran breeding throughout the year. It also appears that species with similar calls breed at different times to lessen confusion.

All frogs must attract mates, and some do this in the most amazing ways. Poison dart frogs of the family Dendrobatidae often use body language. Although this strategy is normally dangerous for small, edible creatures such as frogs, poison dart frogs are very colorful and bold little anurans, as befits their highly toxic nature. Some species jump up and down. One species (*Colostethus trinitatis*) employs especially marvelous choreography. The male turns to face the female, calls boldly, crouches, crawls backward while swinging to one side, leaps upward, and then balances on his hind feet. Audiences of up to eighteen females have been seen watching one male.

Not all frogs call. In Australia, the little frogs (*Taudactylus eungellenis*) wave to each other and make tiny hops and random movements of their front and hind legs. How would such behavior evolve? These frogs live near noisy streams and have no vocal sacs—they have to try something.

FACING PAGE
Wood frog pairs (Rana sylvatica) *in amplexus. The male of this species ignores traditional anuran mate selection protocol and mates with any female nearby. This behavior may be a reaction to the very brief mating season, which in turn is a response to the short northern summers.*
DOUG WECHSLER/ BBC NATURAL HISTORY UNIT

CONSUMMATION FOR A NEW GENERATION

These are unusual courtship practices. In most species, the female frog selects the appropriate calling male and breeding begins. Sometimes the site that the male is calling from is not a good location for laying eggs. He mounts the female anyway, and she ends up carrying him to the nest site.

Nearly all frogs mate by amplexus, the anuran variation on a breeding technique widely used by fish. The principle is that if the two sexes are close enough together, and plenty of eggs and sperm are released into the water at the same time, enough eggs will be fertilized to make the whole thing worthwhile. Most often, the male, who is usually smaller, mounts the female and grips her tightly either in the armpits or just in front of the hind legs. Males of many species have pads on their "thumbs" to aid in gripping. The pressure stimulates the female to release her eggs while the male releases his sperm. The two mix, fertilizing the eggs, which are encapsulated in a gelatinous, transparent sphere. Amplexus also prevents other males from dislodging the male. Afterwards, the female usually leaves and the male goes looking for another mate. Neither sex cares for the eggs or tadpoles. It's a tough start to life.

Amplexus is not quite so reliable as it might seem, however. It appears that frogs and toads have as much trouble telling the sexes apart as people do (distinguishing the sex of frogs, that is). Male toads, in particular, will mount almost anything that resembles a female toad, including dead toads, the wrong species, inanimate objects such as herpetologists' boots, and male frogs. If they have mounted a male toad, the "amplexee" will inform the "amplexor" of his mistake by giving a release click—a series of low-volume clicks or chuckles. Herpetologists can stimulate this call by gripping a male toad by the armpits.

Some female frogs use this call to their advantage. The female North American red-legged frog *Rana aurora* gives release clicks if she is not ready to

AMPLEXUS POSITIONS

NOLA JOHNSTON. ADAPTED

FROM DUELLMAN AND

TRUEB (1986).

release her eggs. The female of the aforementioned carpenter frog who mimics male aggressive calls to draw a male to her does not give release clicks, thereby encouraging amplexus.

Amplexus positions may vary as well. Males of some species grip the female just in front of the hind legs; others straddle the female. In some species, the size difference is so great that the much smaller male simply leans against the female, and in at least one species the male and female face away from each other, with only their rear ends in contact. The rotund rain frogs of the family Microhylidae have arms too short for the male to grasp the female, so they literally "glue" themselves together using secretions from skin glands. The effect has been described as "two golf balls glued together."

A species of the South American harlequin frog (*Atelopus varius*) takes courtship and pair bonding to the extreme. A male harlequin frog defends his territory all year. When a female appears on his turf, he climbs on board and attempts to breed even if the breeding season is many weeks away. And he won't let go. As a result, the female may have to carry the male around on her back for weeks or even months. This is hard on both parties; the female has the extra work of carrying the male, and the male has little chance to feed. Such an extreme commitment to amplexus suggests that a male has few opportunities to meet females.

Few of the thousands of frog species copulate, or internally fertilize their eggs. Only the primitive tailed frog of the Pacific Northwest coast of North America has a "tail," which is really a modified reproductive organ. Tailed frogs breed in

FACING PAGE

An egg mass of the common toad showing only a few of the several thousand laid by a single female. The jelly membrane that protects the eggs is clearly visible. At this stage, eggs are very vulnerable to predators and environmental conditions. KLAUS HONAL

FEW OF THE

THOUSANDS OF

FROG SPECIES

COPULATE, OR

INTERNALLY FER-

TILIZE THEIR

EGGS.

FACING PAGE

Poison dart frogs of the
family Dendrobatidae
generally lay their eggs in
a jellylike mass on land.
When the tadpoles
develop, a guarding adult
will transport them to a
suitable body of water,
such as the tiny pool at the
base of a plant's leaves.

DENNIS SHERIDAN

WILDLIFE

PHOTOGRAPHY

fast-running mountain streams, where copulation is one way to ensure that sperm and eggs are not swept away. Other species facing similar challenges mate with their vents pressed against one another.

In the temperate world, anuran eggs are typically laid in clumps or strings at the surface of the water; in moving water they may be attached to underwater vegetation. The form and location of the egg masses is an important clue to the species that laid them. In the tropics, however, many frog species do not lay their eggs in water. There may be a lack of suitable fish-free breeding areas. Or the product of seventy species' reproductive activities might overwhelm the resources of any breeding pond and attract such a host of predators that survival would rival lotteries in the statistical probability of success. Some species carry their eggs on their backs. The arboreal glass frog (*Centrolenella valerioi*) lays them on leaves that overhang the water so that the tadpoles drop into the pond at hatching. Others, like the flaming poison dart frog (*Dendrobates pumilio*), lay their eggs in moist sites on land and then carry the tadpoles to the water. Many others lay terrestrial eggs that develop into frogs with no tadpole stage.

Foam nests are also common in the tropics. These may be built on land, in branches, or on the water. In most Australian foam nest builders, the female paddles the water with her front feet, bringing trapped air bubbles to the surface. She directs the bubbles backward along her body, where they become trapped in the eggs and jelly she has released. The newly created foam raft protects the eggs as they hang suspended below the surface. African gray treefrogs (*Chiromantis xerampelina*) mate in groups of up to thirty individuals. Each participant joins in beating eggs and seminal fluid into a massive foam nest in branches overhanging the water.

THE GREAT TRANSFORMATION

Most frogs have a tadpole stage that lasts a single season, although it can range anywhere from as few as nine days in species such as spadefoots to several years in tailed frogs. In Europe and North America, the tadpoles of some large frogs, such as bullfrogs, overwinter in this stage, sometimes for two or three winters.

Many tadpoles have an oval body, a finned tail, and a beaklike mouth with primitive teeth. Most are vegetarian grazers on algae. They breathe as fish do, by means of gills. They sometimes form large aggregations, which may help stir up food, increase each tadpole's temperature through mass absorption of sunlight, and even provide some protection from predators both by enhancing the statistical chances that any individual tadpole can avoid being eaten, and in the same way as schools of fish, by having more eyes on the lookout and group movements that may make it harder for predators to aim at a particular target. As tadpoles metamorphose into air breathers, the digestive tract shortens for carnivorous life, the gills are replaced by lungs, the tail is absorbed, legs develop, the head and body change to adult form, and true teeth appear. Metamorphosis normally happens quickly because the transforming frog is very vulnerable to predators at this time, being neither fish nor fowl but being equally unsuited for life on land and in the water.

But there can also be great variation in the form and lifestyle of the tadpoles. Tadpoles of the tailed frog display adaptations that are common in stream tadpoles: thick muscles in their tails; flattened, streamlined bodies; and large mouths, which can generate enough suction to hold them in place on the rocks of fast-flowing mountain streams. For years, the adult of the paradoxical frog of South America (*Pseudis paradoxa*), had never been "seen" until it was discovered that the tadpole was much larger than the adult frog; tadpoles can exceed 20 centimeters (8 inches) in length, whereas adults are rarely more than 7 centimeters (2.75

FACING PAGE
A "herd" of common toad tadpoles, which are probably all from the same egg mass. Toad tadpoles are among the smallest in the frog world and often graze collectively, like a miniature school of fish.
ROBERT McCAW

The moment of transition
from herbivorous tadpole
to carnivorous toadlet
approaches for a young
common toad. Soon the
tail will be absorbed, the
lungs will complete their
development, and the
jaws, tongue, and
gut of a predator will
appear. KLAUS HONAL

inches) in body length. A continent away, the South African frog (*Kassina maculata*) rarely reaches half the size of its tadpoles.

Although most tadpoles are vegetarians, some are carnivorous. Tadpoles of the dwarf clawed frogs of the genus *Hymenochirus* eat small invertebrates by suction. Spineheaded treefrogs (*Anotheca spinosa*) swallow the eggs of other frogs whole. Perhaps the most ferocious of the tadpole carnivores is the spadefoot, which chops up its prey with its teeth. Spadefoots are a good example of both the ecological advantage of eating other animals and the tendency of natural selection to bet on all the horses in a race. That is to say, the natural world is full of seemingly contradictory behaviors, such as herbivores that eat meat; *fratricide* among bird nest mates; or, in the case of spadefoots, adaptive cannibalism. Each of these actions may benefit the survival of the individual animal that employs it.

Spadefoot breeding takes place in a rush. Spadefoots in North America are mostly prairie and desert species that lay their eggs in temporary ponds created by heavy summer rains. Each breeding episode is thus a chance affair, for the ponds may dry up before larval development is complete. In response to crowding and exposure to tiny freshwater shrimp, some individual tadpoles abandon the vegetarian life; they quickly grow larger than their siblings and develop impressive, carnivore-type jaws. As the pond dries up and most tadpoles are faced with starvation followed by dessication and death, the "killer" tadpoles feed on their dead or dying siblings. This increased source of nutrients and energy may provide these cannibals with enough of a growth spurt to complete metamorphosis.

And failure can be the foundation for success. A researcher of spadefoots in one area observed several years of complete failure as the ponds dried up before any tadpole could transform, followed by a year of success. This success could have been influenced, in part or in whole, by the accumulation of nutrients from the decaying tadpoles of previous years.

Parental care can be an element of frog reproduction. African bullfrogs and many members of the neotropical leptodactylid family guard the eggs. Poison dart frogs will look after their eggs and carry the tadpoles. African bullfrogs are famous for the ferocity of the parental instincts. They have been known to attack cranes, other bullfrogs, and even lions and people who approach eggs or larvae. They have also been observed digging escape channels between puddles in ponds that are drying up so that their tadpoles can move to larger bodies of water.

The female of a South American frog (*Leptodactylus bolivianus*) herds her tadpoles by pumping her hindquarters. This action creates currents, which might contain chemical signals. Whatever the stimulus, the tadpoles follow. Midwife toads mate on land, and the male sticks his hind legs into the egg mass, which adheres to him. He then carries the eggs with him as he goes about life until they are ready to hatch. At that point he carries them to water, and they swim away to start their own tadpole stage. Species of several different families of frogs carry their larvae to water-filled hollows.

In a touching display of courage, male poison dart frogs of the species *Colostethus subpunctatus* guard their eggs, which have been laid under stones, from predators. These nurse guards are less than 25 millimeters (1 inch) long. Females of other poison dart frog species lay their eggs in the water-filled hollows of bromeliad plants and feed their tadpoles with unfertilized eggs released from their own bodies. Some species regularly visit the youngsters to deposit more eggs.

Darwin's frog (*Rhinoderma darwinii*) of Chile and Argentina makes dual use of its expandable vocal sacs. The eggs are laid on land, but after a couple of weeks of development, one or more of the attending males take the eggs into their mouths, where they will complete their development in the vocal sacs. Surinam toads lay their eggs in pockets on the female's back. Some young complete their

entire development, from tadpole to adult, in these encapsulated nests. In all but 1 of 450 species of the New World's genus *Eleutherodactylus*, complete metamorphosis takes place in the egg.

For the most unusual, it is usual to examine the fauna of Australia. Perhaps influenced by the overwhelming number of marsupials on that continent, the male marsupial frog (*Assa darlingtoni*) has hip pockets in which he carries tadpoles and metamorphosing juveniles. The eggs are initially laid in a clump on land, and the male remains near the nest. At hatching, the male becomes covered with egg jelly, and some of the tadpoles swim to him and into his pockets. The remaining tadpoles presumably have failed their first and final test. Two to three months later, the pouch-borne tadpoles emerge as fully developed frogs.

But the most bizarre are the gastric brooding frogs (*Rheobatrachus silus*), which live in fast-flowing creeks in the Australian rain forest. After egg laying, the female swallows some of the eggs, which complete their tadpole development in her stomach. No one has ever seen this rare—and possibly extinct—anuran swallow the eggs, but the presence of growing tadpoles can be detected by the distended stomach. Development takes at least six weeks. In the later stages, internal crowding is so severe that the lungs collapse and the frog must breathe through her skin alone. Birthing is spread over a few days: the female frog comes to the surface and opens her mouth; the tadpole pauses on her tongue and then swims out into the real world. This is a unique process, and it is not clearly understood what process shuts off the production of acid in the female's stomach so that the young are not digested.

Whatever the process, at the end of the reproductive cycle the surviving young have become frogs. Perhaps they climbed out of their father's hip pockets or his vocal sacs or swam out of their mother's mouth or, more likely, metamorphosed on their own either in the pond or directly from the egg. And a lot of other species have been waiting for this dramatic moment.

FOOD
Chapter Four
OR FOE

It appears that almost anything will eat an amphibian!
—KENNETH R. PORTER, *Herpetology*

The unusual strategies that frogs employ to produce the next generation reflect a kind of reproductive desperation. Anurans of many species produce thousands of eggs that are left exposed and unguarded. In the temperate world, breeding often involves large numbers of adults crowding together in confined bodies of water in ferocious competition for mates and egg-laying sites. This desperation is justified, for very few frogs live long enough to even have the chance to find a mate. Small, relatively defenseless creatures like anurans are fuel for the ecosystems they inhabit. They represent an enormous quantity of energy that is stored efficiently—as a result of ectothermy—and is available for other organisms when alternative food sources may be scarce. I once suggested to a colleague that if there really is such a thing as reincarnation, and if you are given a choice, don't choose to be a frog for your next life. Dale correctly noted, however, that there might be an upside to such a choice, as it probably wouldn't be long before you got to choose again.

For most frogs, the breeding season is their most vulnerable time. They must gather together in large numbers and make a lot of noise—a recipe for attracting

FACING PAGE

Leopard frog in quest of a dragonfly meal. BIANCA LAVIES/NGS IMAGE COLLECTION

VERY FEW FROGS

LIVE LONG

ENOUGH TO EVEN

HAVE THE CHANCE

TO FIND

A MATE. SMALL,

RELATIVELY

DEFENSELESS

CREATURES LIKE

ANURANS ARE

FUEL FOR THE

ECOSYSTEMS

THEY INHABIT.

predators. They combat this situation in whatever ways are open to them. They may, like chorus frogs and other northern temperate species, breed very early in the year, when perhaps fewer predators are around. Many breed at night, eliminating the daytime predators. The season may be quite short, a few weeks at most, and so predators do not have the opportunity to gather in large numbers. The nature of their great choruses makes it difficult to locate and pinpoint an individual frog. If a calling male detects something predator-sized approaching, he immediately falls silent and may take cover in the aquatic vegetation. As a result, the hunter can end up always pursuing the frog calling just ahead rather than the silent one who is almost within reach. A personal note: this technique is very effective on herpetologists.

But nothing always works. Defense strategies employed by individuals may reduce the numbers of frogs that are taken, and thereby coincidentally ensure that enough have the chance to breed to sustain the species, but for each frog it is like a roulette wheel. The wheel always stops on a number, and that frog is eaten, but the game only allows for a few spins before it ends and the frogs silently disperse. The defenses only succeed in making the wheel spin longer before coming to rest on some little anuran packet of protein.

In the tropics, as always, a few layers of complexity must be added to the roulette analogy. First, there are far more wheels with many more numbers on them. The tropical breeding season may last for many months and involve many species, each of whom employs a different defensive strategy. Some may call from the water, some from beneath the water, others from along the shore or the nearby vegetation, and others from various heights in the trees. This situation forces predators to choose which frog type to go after; you can't hunt tree-calling frogs from the water.

Second, there are many more eyes and ears searching for frog meals. Our

FACING PAGE

Red-eyed treefrogs
(Agalchnis callidryas)
demonstrate the variety of
niches in the tropics. The
base of a tropical flower
provides both an excellent
hiding place and a point
from which to ambush
pollinating insects.
ART WOLFE

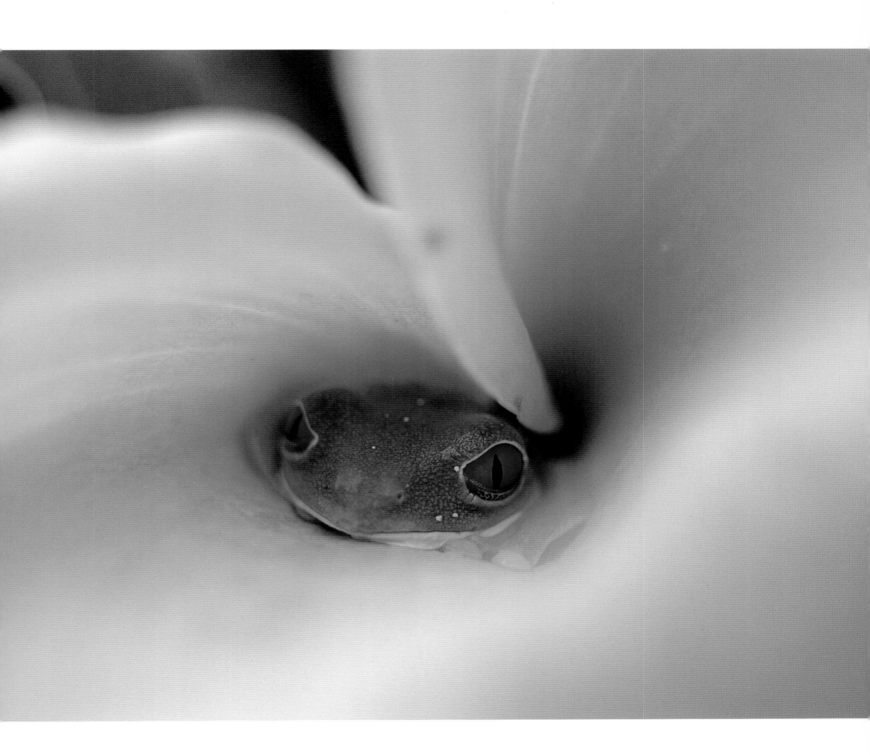

roulette wheel is now just one of many at a very large casino, and there are lots of players.

FROG FOES

Who are these predators? Dr. Porter is right—it seems to be just about everybody. Frog eggs, tadpoles, and aquatic adults are favorite meals for fish around the world. Predatory aquatic insects such as diving beetles prey heavily on tadpoles. Frogs that live in or near the water are often hunted by wading birds, such as herons; by a host of snake species; by many small to medium-sized mammals, such as raccoons, opossums, and skunks; and by other, larger frogs. Tiny spadefoots that have just transformed from the tadpole stage may be ambushed by the hooked mandibles of horsefly larvae buried in the soil near the breeding pond. In the tropics, additional dangers come from unexpected sources; there are bats that specialize in hunting frogs, which they locate by the call. Tropical frogs may be caught in webs and eaten by spiders. One tropical hawk extracts frogs from their daytime hiding spots in the leaves of bromeliads.

Frogs have a variety of techniques to help them make it through the day and night. The first defense is to avoid detection. Many frogs have cryptic coloration that makes it difficult for a predator to see them. The North American gray treefrog (*Hyla versicolor*) has a mottled gray pattern that quite strikingly matches the lichen-encrusted branches and tree trunks that are its usual home. Aquatic frogs are usually green or brown to mimic the dominant colors of water and plants. A few species even have bony protruding structures that disrupt their smooth outline and and make it even more difficult to identify them as frogs rather than pieces of the earth or a plant.

Detection alone does not mean a capture. If the predator succeeds in locating the frog—and predators have spent eons developing frog-detection techniques—

they still have to catch it. The anuran has two choices: it can run away or stand its ground. Species that run away have powerful legs. Some make a single leap into the nearby water, whereas others make a series of straight jumps and then stop. Still others jump in an erratic zigzag manner before suddenly freezing. Freezing is the key element in the zigzag leapers, for the predator's eyes tend to continue scanning to the point where the next jump should have taken the jumper. Personal experience confirms that it can be amazingly difficult to find a motionless frog, even when you saw where it landed. Treefrogs and some other species add a further refinement to the leap. They have bright coloration, often orange, yellow, or red, on the portion of their thighs that is not visible when they are at rest. When they leap, this bright flash appears as their legs extend and then magically disappears when the frog lands and assumes its normal at-rest position. Presumably the predator's eyes are drawn to the location of the burst of color rather than to the now concealed anuran.

Frogs that lack the tools for flight—large, powerful hind legs—must stand their ground in a confrontation, and some do so confidently. Most toads contain within the warts and glands on their backs and sides powerful toxins that at the least make them distasteful for many potential predators and, in the most severe circumstances, may cause death. Other animals learn of this danger early, so only a few species specialize in eating toads. For these, toads employ a defense common to many of the larger anurans; they swell themselves up and often arch their bodies so that their head—the preferable part for a snake to grasp—is touching the ground. Other poisonous frogs freely advertise their dangerous skin. The bright, enamel-like colors of the poison dart frogs, which are some of the most beautiful creatures in the world, inform predators of their extremely dangerous skin toxins. Aboriginal people in South and Central America use these toxins to poison the darts with which they hunt monkeys in the rain forest. The more lethal

FACING PAGE

Predators such as this European grass snake (Natrix natrix) *that are not deterred by the venom of the common toad may be discouraged by the posturing-and-swelling-up defense. The probable message: "I am far too large for you to eat!"*

TONY PHELPS/BBC NATURAL HISTORY UNIT

species contain enough of these compounds to kill an adult human. Other toxic species lack the bold, always visible coloration of the poison dart frogs. These species, such as the fire-bellied toads of Europe and Asia, hide their warning colorations on their undersides, and so they must contort their bodies to provide predators with the information that will make them go away.

There are other close-in defenses. A number of harmless frog species bear a striking resemblance to the poisonous ones; mimicry may be at work in these cases. Some species play dead when confronted at close quarters by a serious predator. They may simply let their bodies go limp; some keep their limbs tight against their bodies and lie motionless on their backs. At least one species tucks its legs under its body, closes its eyes, and lets its tongue dangle from its mouth.

Other frogs take a more aggressive approach. Some bite, or at least threaten to bite, with mouths open. A frog of the New World tropics, *Caudiverbera caudiverbera*, does the Full Monty, inflating itself, rising high on its legs, emitting loud cries, and jumping at the predator. North American bullfrogs and other species utter loud, very unfroglike cries when grabbed by predators such as snakes (or humans). One explanation that has been offered is that these are warning calls for the other frogs, but it is unlikely that bullfrogs (or any frogs for that matter) are so altruistic as to put others first. It is more likely that the cry is a reaction to stress and fear or that it is intended to startle the predator into releasing the animal. And it is very startling. Another theory suggests that the cry is meant to attract other, larger predators that might attack, or at least distract, the first, allowing the frog to escape.

A footnote to the discussion of frog toxins. All of these poisons are for defense, as opposed to the venoms of cobras or rattlesnakes, which are used to subdue prey and only secondarily for defense. People are not in danger from handling a toxic toad, provided that they wash their hands thoroughly after touching

A FROG OF THE

NEW WORLD

TROPICS,

CAUDIVERBERA

CAUDIVERBERA,

DOES THE FULL

MONTY, INFLATING

ITSELF, RISING

HIGH ON ITS

LEGS, EMITTING

LOUD CRIES, AND

JUMPING AT THE

PREDATOR.

the animal and have no cuts or wounds, and of course, that they don't eat it. No frogs have adapted their toxic secretions for use in subduing their prey.

GREAT WET HUNTERS OF MARSH AND FOREST

Frogs are predators. A handful of species have been recorded eating plant material, including small fruits, but these are very much the exception. Ninety-nine percent of adult anurans eat other animals. To be prey for a frog, the animal must be of a size that can be overpowered by the frog's mouth alone. The front legs of anurans are not powerful and do not have claws. Their feet are of no use in capturing prey or in tearing it into bite-sized chunks. Nor are their small teeth strong enough to rip the prey into pieces. This absence of supporting weapons thus places a lot of responsibility on the frog mouth. A frog must capture prey using only its mouth, the whole prey must fit inside the mouth, and the frog must be able to swallow the sometimes large and actively struggling animal with its mouth alone. And what a mouth it is.

The great gape of most frog mouths enables them to take on surprisingly large prey and provides a base for their specialized long-range weapon, the tongue. "Long-range," of course, is a relative term, and no frog's tongue is comparable in length to a chameleon's, for example. The frog tongue at rest lies folded on the floor of the mouth. It is normally attached at the front of the lower jaw rather than at the back, as in people and a host of other animals. This forward attachment provides the maximum range for launching a feature of considerable importance in capturing flying insects. As the tongue lies folded in the mouth, the sticky portion at the tip of the tongue faces up. When prey is within range, the frog opens its mouth and flips its tongue at the target. The prey is stuck to the tongue, which is quickly flipped back into the mouth. The action is very fast, sometimes a matter

FACING PAGE

The small front feet of this green frog (Rana clamitans) *are of little use in overpowering prey or even in aiding swallowing. The prey must be overcome by mouth alone.*

JOE MCDONALD

In this illustration, the
shaded portion of the tongue
is sticky and is flicked at the
prey to make the capture.
NOLA JOHNSTON

FACING PAGE

This common toad is not
falling asleep or feeling
smug. It is using the
muscles in back of its
eyes to help force prey
down its throat.
GAY BUMGARNER

of milliseconds, and a human observer might not even realize that the tongue was involved. Once inside those jaws, the prey is swallowed as quickly as possible, sometimes aided by contractions of the eye muscles, which help push the prey down the throat.

Most frogs employ one of two basic hunting strategies. The most common strategy is the sit-and-wait technique. This technique is straightforward; choose a site frequented by prey species, count on your coloration and immobility for camouflage, and ambush anything of the right size that passes close enough. If the prey is near but not close enough, the frog may slowly lean forward or take a cautious step or two to close the range. Smaller, slender anurans such as the poison dart frogs actively forage through their habitat searching for appropriately sized, relatively slow-moving prey.

Some frogs have appended refinements on to the sit-and-wait method. The horned frogs (genus *Ceratophrys*) of the New World tropics use their toes as lures to draw prey close to their camouflaged mouths. Ornate horned frogs (*Ceratophrys ornata*) have bright yellow toes on their hind feet, which they lift above their hindquarters. From frog eye level and in front, the yellow toes may be mistaken for a small flower, fruit, or insect resting above a nondescript piece of the rain forest floor, an error in identification that can have serious consequences.

Anurans eat almost anything moving that fits into their mouths. For most frogs, "anything" means insects and many other invertebrates. But give a frog a little size and you'll see the ferocious carnivore that lives inside. Large frogs such as North American and African bullfrogs, as well as South American horned frogs, regularly eat small mammals, birds, other frogs, turtles, and even snakes. One African bullfrog ate seventeen newborn cobras, and another attacked a small chicken. Other prey not normally thought of as frog food include marine crabs and snails. Frogs generally locate their prey by sight, but some species clearly

THE GREAT GAPE

OF MOST FROG

MOUTHS ENABLES

THEM TO TAKE ON

SURPRISINGLY

LARGE PREY AND

PROVIDES A BASE

FOR THEIR

SPECIALIZED

LONG-RANGE

WEAPON,

THE TONGUE.

possess a sense of smell. Marine toads (*Bufo marinus*) also called cane toads, will eat vegetable scraps, pet food, and carrion.

A favorite example of opportunism in anurans comes from the southeastern United States, where an ornithologist was studying cedar waxwings, colorful starling-sized birds that flock together in winter and are partial to berries. The researcher was watching a large flock of waxwings gorging themselves on berries and making frequent trips to a nearby lake for a drink. After a time he noticed the presence of numerous large bullfrogs along the edge of the lake, many of which had strangely distended bodies. It did not take long to discover the cause; the frogs were patiently ambushing the birds as they came for a drink. If frogs were the size of dogs, we would never go near the water!

There are, as always with anurans, exceptions to every rule. The marvels of the anuran tongue are denied to the completely aquatic pipids (members of the family Pipidae). Pipids have no tongues and basically suck in food. When the prey is large, some species use their "fingers" to aid in swallowing. Observations of captive pipids reveal that they use their toes to "feel" for prey in murky water and then use their fingers to sweep it into their mouths. Many burrowing anurans feed on ants and termites and other underground creatures. In the confined space below the soil surface, tongue flipping is not very practical. Some species solve this problem by slipping their rod-shaped tongues in and out through a small groove between the upper and lower jaws. Others, like burrowing toads (*Rhinophrynus dorsalis*), hunt at the surface by locating termite nests and trails.

As a final footnote to predators and prey, I must mention the story of Fang. Fang was a gray treefrog, which I kept as a pet for a few months. I must add that anurans make mediocre pets—they are very inactive and may be difficult to find food for—and I advise against the practice. Fang had been captured because he displayed the opportunism that characterizes many of the most successful species.

FACING PAGE

The business end of a large African bullfrog (Pyxicephalus adspersus), *or "Pixie," as herpetologists sometimes refer to this species. This one is upset; it has inflated itself and may lunge forward to bite. Any prey-sized animal seeing this view is in deep trouble.*

GEORGE GRALL/

NGS IMAGE COLLECTION

He was on a window of our house patiently hunting nocturnal insects that had been drawn to our house light. He was a quiet pet, only calling on occasional warm, humid nights, except for feeding time. When I arrived with the plastic jar containing moths I had captured, Fang would immediately become agitated and start scrambling along the branches in his terrarium. I would usually remove the lid of the terrarium, deposit the container of moths, remove the container lid, quickly replace the mesh cage top, and let the games begin. Watching Fang stalk and capture those moths was my first extended chance to study anuran hunting techniques.

But what lingers most clearly in my mind after a passage of at least twenty years is Fang's commitment to his work. Apparently Fang felt the same way about moths as I feel about pizza. He simply could not stop eating them even when his stomach was distended and sagging from the presence of three or four large moths. It was a pathetic but amusing sight to see him try to haul himself within range of yet another moth, sometimes with a moth wing still protruding from his mouth. I was greatly impressed by his commitment.

THE FUTURE OF
Chapter Five
THE ORDER ANURA

By the late 1980s second-order effects [of clear cutting] could be seen spreading through the food web. With the peccaries gone, there were no wallows in which temporary forest pools could form. Without the pools, three species of Phyllomedusa *frogs failed to breed and disappeared.*

—E.O. WILSON, on the Manaus Experiment,
in *The Diversity of Life*

Information about frogs can be difficult to acquire, for anurans are diverse and secretive, and their populations are in constant flux. It doesn't help that the greatest diversity and abundance of anurans are found in the tropics, while herpetologists are concentrated in the temperate world. In addition, relatively little information has been collected over a long enough period of time for patterns to become discernible. Of the four thousand or so species of living anurans, scientists have a good knowledge base for a few hundred species at most.

There is enough information to suggest that a bleak future may lie ahead for many frog species. Declines are simply too widespread and significant to be explained by coincidence. But the order Anura has a long history of natural selection on its side. Frogs are not frail things. And even in the midst of a crisis, some species prosper.

NEW WORLDS TO CONQUER

Over two hundred million years of adaptability hasn't ended. The world still presents anurans with new environments and circumstances, and frogs still respond.

FACING PAGE
A bullfrog (Rana catesbeiana) *where it shouldn't be—in Sonoma County, California. This eastern North American species has been introduced to many new locations in North America and around the world. And where it has successfully adapted, native species have usually suffered.* MICHAEL SEWELL/VISUAL PURSUIT

FROGS ARE NOT

FRAIL THINGS. AND

EVEN IN THE

MIDST OF A

CRISIS. SOME

SPECIES PROSPER.

Humans have been the major cause of changes in frog environments in recent times. Dispersal is a good example; anurans formerly had to travel by their own means to find new territories. But for some species, humans have played an active role. African clawed frogs, green frogs, bullfrogs, and other species have been introduced in new areas both accidentally and intentionally. Introduced by accident, when captive individuals escaped into the wild, or for science or for economic reasons, all have established themselves on new continents or in new countries or just in new parts of the same country. They have proven to be quite adaptable, and many populations are increasing even as an alarming number of anuran populations are declining. But one species surpasses all the rest in any measurement of successful immigration. It also illustrates the problems that can occur when a species is introduced to a new area.

The cane toad (*Bufo marinus*) is one of the largest toads in the world; a very large individual can be 24 centimeters (9½ inches) long and weigh well over a kilogram (2 pounds). These toads are native to northern South America and all of Central America and range as far north as southern Texas. They were the first amphibian I encountered in Leticia, Colombia, on the Amazon. I was sitting in a lawn chair overlooking a small courtyard, when a very large toad *walked* across the grass. It was an impressive sight and set the tone for my experience of herpetology in the tropics. If cane toads had stayed in their home countries, they would have remained unnoticed by the world at large—just an amazingly big toad playing its role in the almost inconceivable complexity of the rain forest.

But early in the twentieth century cane toads were recruited for work in other areas. In many ways, they were ideal immigrants: they had jobs lined up, protecting agricultural crops from insect pests; they would cost little to settle; and they would do work that the local inhabitants couldn't or wouldn't do. They had already been introduced to several islands in the Caribbean as biological controls before the middle of the eighteenth century, but their first big job came in Puerto Rico. They were introduced to this Caribbean island in 1920 specifically to control beetles that fed on the sugar cane plant, a vital part of the island's economy. By 1932, cane toads were stars in the sugar cane growers' world. The beetles were no longer a serious pest, and the hero of the hour was a large, lumpy, gray toad that performed its work efficiently and at no cost to government or farmer. Although the extent of the success that can really be attributed to cane toads is uncertain, even the respected, notoriously restrained journal *Nature* trumpeted: "Toads save sugar crop." In the distance could be faintly heard the sound of agronomists scrambling for the bandwagon.

In 1935, R.W. Montgomery returned from Hawaii, where cane toads were introduced in 1932, with 101 toads. By 1939, toads had been released at a number of locations along the coast of Australia's Queensland State amid forecasts of the end of the reign of terror by destructive cane beetles. That was sixty years ago.

Today the cane toad is an animal weed like the starling and the brown rat. It is a contented resident of much of Queensland and is making inroads into other areas. As a predator on cane beetles, it was a failure. The beetles that it was meant to feed on can fly, so on many occasions, they were not available to the terrestrial toad. But cane toads found other prey to their liking—lots of other prey, including native marsupials and frogs. They also displaced the local anurans at the breeding ponds. In the presence of abundant food and the absence of predators, cane toad populations increased exponentially. Those creatures who tried to prey on cane toads encountered their highly toxic skin secretions, often with fatal results. On the substantial list of native Australian animals that have died as a result of biting cane toads are Tasmanian devils, kookaburras, goannas (large lizards), and several of the world's most dangerously venomous snakes, including death adders, brown snakes, and tiger snakes.

Finding the cane fields too exposed, some toads have taken up residence in many towns and cities, where they gather near the light from houses and street lamps to feed on insects. Part of *Bufo marinus*'s clever plan may be to supplant the dog as a favored house pet. A number of dogs have died from mouthing toads, and many toads have been observed eating dog food.

Massive campaigns have been undertaken both to reduce the population and to prevent the spread of cane toads into new areas. Motorists have been encouraged to run over toads. A University of Queensland researcher has estimated that over 200 *tons* of cane toads are squelched annually on Queensland roads. Brisbane City Council has promoted cane toad busting as a fun activity for the whole family, and trips to Hawaii have been awarded for the highest total. The cruel days of toad bashing with golf clubs and cricket clubs are over; the animals are now collected and killed humanely by freezing.

These campaigns have had limited success, and it seems clear that cane toads have become yet another amazing—if unwanted—addition to the weird and wonderful fauna of Australia. But if the cane toad is, in an evolutionary sense, an anuran success story, it is more than offset by the losses on other fronts.

THE MYSTERY OF THE DISAPPEARING ANURANS

In Australia, the gastric brooding frog was last seen in 1985. Granted, a frog that raises its young in its stomach might seem an evolutionary mistake anyway, but this species has since been joined in probable extinction by the mountain mist frog (*Litoria nyakalensis*), the northern tinker-frog (*Taudactylus rheophilus*), and the sharp-snouted day frog (*Taudactylus acutirostris*). The southern day frog (*Taudactylus diurnus*) has not been seen since 1979. Many other populations have severely declined.

The brilliant golden toad (*Bufo periglenes*), which seemed well protected in the Monteverde Cloud Forest Reserve of Costa Rica, has not been known to breed since 1987, and what are believed to be the last two individuals were spotted only a few years ago. The harlequin frog has nearly vanished from the same range.

Three species of *Eleutherodactylus* may now be extinct in Puerto Rico, and another 10 percent of the frog fauna is at risk. In one area of Parque Nacional Pico Bonito in Honduras, four (25 percent) of the frog species appear to be extirpated (gone from a particular location) or extinct (gone forever).

In 1992, biologists resurveyed thirty-eight sites along an east-west transect in Yosemite National Park originally surveyed for vertebrates by a team from 1915 through 1919. The results of this study document a decline in a whole anuran fauna across a large, diverse region that is protected from development and habitat destruction. Three species were not found at any of the previously surveyed sites; many others had decreased significantly in numbers. Only the introduced bullfrog showed any indication of increasing abundance.

Elsewhere in California, the mountain yellow-legged frog (*Rana muscosa*) and the Yosemite toad (*Bufo canorus*) are missing from most of the Sierra Nevada. The arroyo toad (*Bufo californicus*) of Southern California has vanished from three-fourths of its range. The red-legged frog (*Rana aurora*) that once lived throughout Southern California is down to one remote area of Riverside County.

In Canada, there have been major declines, especially in western Canada, but few extirpations, including the leopard frog in southeastern British Columbia and the cricket frog (*Acris crepitans*) on Pelee Island in Ontario. The latter was abundant as recently as the 1970s but has not been observed in the last decade.

In the 1980s, reports of declining amphibian populations from virtually every continent in the world began to worry scientists. The most alarming trend was the international scope of the disappearances and declines and the fact that many

TODAY THE CANE TOAD IS AN ANIMAL WEED LIKE THE STARLING AND THE BROWN RAT.

of these apparent crises were occurring in parks and other protected areas. Backed by many governments, the International Union for the Conservation of Nature set up the Declining Amphibian Populations Task Force in 1992. National task forces were established in many countries, all to answer the question "Why?" The answers to date are almost all unequivocally varied and partial.

There is no evidence of a single smoking gun, but given the diversity of frogs and the areas they live in, this is not surprising. In many cases, the cause seems straightforward. The dramatic loss of wetlands in industrialized countries, and now increasingly in the developing countries, may be the greatest single factor in declining amphibian populations. Many people remember the field or pond from their youth that is now gone, covered by housing or asphalt. That pond probably supported frogs. Industrial activities such as mining and logging also remove habitat.

Our infrastructure of roads and highways can also cause disaster. Frogs sometimes migrate great distances to and from hibernating and breeding areas. During migrations, huge numbers may be killed crossing roads, as the following article illustrates:

TOAD CROSSING

Every year in Britain about 300,000 toads get squashed while crossing roads to get to their breeding pools. Hundreds of volunteers all over England are coming to the rescue by spending their evenings ferrying the warty amphibians across the roads in buckets.

One of the volunteers, Mick Durant, explained how he got involved in the toad rescue:

"I just went down the lane one day when it was wet and warm to buy a packet of cigarettes, and I saw all these poor little animals on the ground just splattered everywhere."

A familiar sight in wetlands, meadows, and biology labs across North America, even leopard frogs, such as this northern leopard frog (Rana pipiens), *have suffered declines in local areas and have disappeared from portions of Western Canada.* SCOT STEWART

"I mean, I'm a builder and builders are supposed to be strong. But driving home one night and seeing all the dead toads, I just sat in my car and cried."

—*Associated Press*, March 1994

Although caution signs, diversion fences, and tunnels have been installed in some locations to reduce the carnage, the same tragedy unfolds annually in much of Europe and North America. Working for the National Parks in Canada, I was once part of a biological road survey along a two-lane road that marked the northern boundary of a national park. At regular intervals over thirty days and nights my partner and I slowly cruised the approximately 5-kilometer (3-mile) stretch of highway, stopping to note what was either "alive-on-road" or "dead-on-road." It was a frightening and depressing experience, for we found representation from almost every animal grouping: mammals, birds, reptiles, amphibians, and invertebrates. We would stop to examine a large snapping turtle, shell crushed but still alive, or a gravid fox snake lured to her death by the comfort of the warm asphalt. But when we shone our flashlight beyond the body being inspected, we realized that death happened on a wide scale, for everywhere we looked were flattened remnants—too flat to be detected without close examination. The thousands of insects were followed in numbers by the frogs. At each stop we would remove the corpses in order to avoid counting them again, and each subsequent survey would reveal their replacements. It was an unintended, unending war of attrition.

So many human activities have a negative impact on anurans. The introduction of trout and other predatory fish species often has a devastating impact on frog populations because anurans are desired prey for fish. These introductions are considered the biggest threat to amphibians in the upper Midwestern states. Similarly, the introduction of large predatory frogs such as bullfrogs, which has occurred throughout North America, can cause havoc for the local anurans.

Many countries are examining the use of herbicides and pesticides because of their effect on frogs and their tadpoles. For example, the Australian government has banned eighty-four herbicide products from use near water because of their effect on anurans. Many herbicides have detergent compounds that interfere with gill respiration in tadpoles. Frog eggs and tadpoles often live in small, shallow bodies of water, where they are especially vulnerable to toxins.

Some scientists blame acid precipitation for declines. Even small amounts of toxic compounds carried by the wind, rain, and snow might deal fatal blows to animals that tend to breathe through their moist skins. Studies in Oregon suggest that the thinning ozone layer has increased ultraviolet radiation, causing damage to the egg masses of several anuran species, including the western toad and the Cascades frog (*Rana cascadae*).

An explanation for one decline may be in the offing. Fungal infections appear to be the cause of mortality in frogs in montane rain forests in Australia and Central America, although no explanation has been found for why this apparently new, virulent form should appear almost simultaneously in areas many thousands of kilometers apart. Perhaps the animals were already weakened or stressed by other factors, such as habitat deterioration.

There is, in short, no single clear-cut explanation for most declines in frog populations. This is not unexpected; a former professor of mine liked to say that for every complex problem, there is a simple, straightforward *wrong* answer. Some scientists question whether the crisis is real or whether new data have exposed natural fluctuations in populations. In spite of appearances, frogs are pretty tough characters who have survived millions of years of climate change and other major environmental events. To look at a cane toad in contrast to the Costa Rican golden toad suggests that perhaps there are simply evolutionary winners and losers. Perhaps.

THE FUTURE OF THE FROG

Although it might seem futile, there are things that an individual can do to help anurans. In North America and other areas, there are amphibian monitoring programs that depend in part on amateur volunteers. Through such programs, you can learn more about the anurans in your area and take steps to make your property frog friendly. Herpetologists and other scientists have made solving the mystery of declining amphibians their main research goal. Many countries have established specific task forces to meet this challenge. You can contact park and wildlife management agencies to obtain information and advice and to find out what role you can play in this crisis. On the Internet, search for "froglog" to learn about past and present research into anuran disappearances by amphibian task forces around the world.

I have left to last the two great roles that frogs may play in our world. First, they consume incredible volumes of insects and are, in turn, eaten by an amazing variety of other animals. Their disappearance would have—and is having—a huge impact on these other organisms. Second, frogs are indicators of the condition of our environment and a measure of its quality. They do not go first when things get tough. It is the grizzly bear and the Eurasian lion that first slip away from the scene. Frogs persist. In an account of a particularly horrible battle in World War One, I read of the horrors of constant artillery shelling and the miserable life of a soldier in the water-logged trenches. But the author noted that during pauses in the firing, the soldiers were distracted by the calls of thousands of frogs opportunistically starting a new generation in flooded shell craters.

If there is a lesson to be drawn, it is that we should not be too certain that because frogs are now declining in many parts of the world, they will be the first to go.

As teenagers, a friend and I used to explore the natural areas near our homes in quest of "herps"—amphibians and reptiles. We would pick up any toad we saw and study its expression, which seemed to exude hostility and arrogance. I am still fascinated by the expression on a toad's face and all the history that hides behind it. And I would not bet against a creature with such an attitude and sense of self.

Whenever toad passed one of these ponds
He would plunk himself down
And call out, "Earth,
Let us celebrate a birthday,
For though you are large, and round,
I am beautiful, and a wonder,
And can walk wherever I please."

—SUSAN FROMBERG SCHAEFFER, *Narcissus Toad*

FOR FURTHER READING

In the last two decades, there has been a great increase in the number of books that deal with amphibians. The books listed here are especially fine examples of the range of information available.

Amphibian Biology

Duellman, W. E., and L. Trueb. 1986. *The Biology of Amphibians.* Baltimore, Md.: Johns Hopkins University Press. A comprehensive illustrated reference book that fully explores the biology of amphibians. The standard technical reference.

Green, D. M., ed. 1997. *Amphibians in Decline: Canadian Studies of a Global Problem.* St. Louis, Mo.: Society for the Study of Amphibians and Reptiles Publishers. The first volume of a report to the IUCN Declining Amphibian Populations Task Force discussing population studies, status reports, and studies and reviews of potential causes of amphibian declines.

Stebbins, R. C., and N. W. Cohen. 1995. *A Natural History of Amphibians.* Princeton, N.J.: Princeton University Press. A comprehensive resource introducing the natural history of amphibians throughout the world. Very readable.

Field Guides

There are many superb field guides available throughout the world. Field guides offer much more than tools for identifying individual species. Tucked into the brief descriptions are concise summaries of the life history of each species.

Arnold, E. N.; J. A. Burton; and D. W. Ovenden. 1978. *A Field Guide to the Reptiles and Amphibians of Britain and Europe.* Glasgow: William Collins Sons. An excellent guide. A new edition is scheduled for publication in 2000.

Behler, J. L., and F. W. King. 1979. *The Audubon Society Field Guide to North American Reptiles and Amphibians.* New York: Alfred A. Knopf. A pocket-sized field guide for all of North America. Unlike most field guides, uses photographs rather than illustrations.

Conant, R., and J. T. Collins. 1998. *A Field Guide to Reptiles and Amphibians of Eastern and Central North America.* 3rd ed. Peterson Field Guide Series. Boston: Houghton Mifflin. The standard guide for eastern North America.

Corkran, C. C., and C. Thomas. 1996. *Amphibians of Oregon, Washington and British Columbia.* Edmonton: Lone Pine. One of the finest regional guides available. Filled with information about habitats, species during all stages of their lives, and tips for studying and photographing amphibians.

FACING PAGE

Hyla arborea *in flight.*

CSABA FORRÁSY

Stebbins, R. C. 1998. *A Field Guide to Western Reptiles and Amphibians*. 3rd ed. Peterson Field Guide Series. Boston: Houghton Mifflin. The standard guide for western North America.

Human-Anuran Connections

Caduto, M. J., and J. Bruchac. 1991. *Native Stories from Keepers of the Earth*. Saskatoon, Sask.: Fifth House Publishers. A collection of aboriginal stories from North American aboriginal groups that illustrate the entwined relationships between human beings and nature.

Degraaff, R. M. 1991. *The Book of the Toad*. Rochester, Vt.: Park Street Press. A natural and magical history of toad-human relations.

Ferguson, G. 1996. *Spirits of the Wild: The World's Great Nature Myths*. New York: Clarkson Potter. A collection of myths and stories from around the world that include a wide range of animals.

Lewis, S. 1989. *Cane Toads: An Unnatural History*. New York: A Dolphin Book / Bantam Doubleday Dell Publishing Group. A book that is both humorous and sobering and that looks at how an introduced species, imported as a form of pest control, has become the pest.

Morgan, A. 1995. *Toads and Toadstools*. Berkeley: Celestial Arts. The natural history, folklore, and cultural oddities of a strange association.

Shaw, R. 1972. *The Frog Book*. New York: Frederick Warne & Co. An illustrated compilation of poems, fables, and stories about frogs.

General Herpetology

Cogger, H. G., and R. G. Zweifel. 1998. *Reptiles and Amphibians*. 2nd ed. New York: Smithmark Publishers. A comprehensive illustrated guide by international experts discussing habitat, species, and the evolution of reptiles and amphibians. Intended for a lay audience.

Pough, F. H.; R. M. Andrews; J. E. Cadle; M. L. Crump; A. H. Savitzky; and K. D. Wells. 1998. *Herpetology*. Upper Saddle River, N. J.: Prentice-Hall. An advanced textbook reviewing and exploring the latest research on reptiles and amphibians from a diversity of disciplines.

Zug, G. R. 1993. *Herpetology: An Introductory Biology of Amphibians and Reptiles*. San Diego: Academic Press. A herpetology book designed for advanced undergraduates that explores the biology and current research of amphibians and reptiles.

General Biology

Wilson, E. O. 1992. *The Diversity of Life*. Cambridge, Mass.: The Belknap Press of Harvard University Press. An exploration of the biodiversity of the natural world and an acknowledgment that preservation and the economic development of the world's resources can and must work together. A classic work that no one interested in the state of our natural world should be without.

APPENDIX: FROG FAMILIES

Taxonomy is the classification of organisms based on their natural relationships. For centuries, this work has been based on anatomical features—the size, shape, and number of bones, organs, and so on. In recent years, however, a branch of taxonomy known as phylogenetics has dramatically changed the way we look at species and at the larger organizing systems, such as families and orders. Phylogeneticists classify organisms through numerical data such as DNA sequences. As a result, the evolutionary relationships between organisms are better understood, and new species may be recognized.

Taxonomy is a living science and, like all disciplines, is based on incorporating new information into new theories and evaluating the results. Not surprisingly, there is disagreement among scientists about what might seem to be basic questions such as how many species there are. The following description of the families of frogs alive today follows a recent review in *Herpetology* by Pough et al. (1998). Like frog species, some families of frogs have no common name.

One last taxonomical note: these families belong to the order Anura, which includes all living species of tailless amphibian. The order Salientia includes all living amphibians and their extinct relatives. In other words, all anurans are part of the order Salientia, but only living salientians belong to the order Anura.

Family	Common Name	Genera	Approximate No. of Species	Distribution
Ascaphidae	Tailed frogs	1	1	North America
Leiopelmatidae		1	3	New Zealand
Bombinatoridae	Fire-bellied toads	2	8	Europe, Asia
Discoglossidae		2	5	Europe, Africa
Pelobatidae		10	95	North America, Europe, Asia, Africa
Pelodytidae		1	2	Europe, Asia
Rhinophrynidae	Burrowing toads	1	1	North America, Central America
Pipidae	Pipids	5	30	South America, Africa
Allophrynidae		1	1	South America
Brachycephalidae		2	3	South America
Bufonidae	Toads	33	380	North America, Central America, South America, Europe, Africa, Asia
Heleophrynidae	Ghost frogs	1	5	Africa
Leptodactylidae*		49	900	North America, Central America, South America
Myobatrachidae		21	110	Australia and adjacent islands
Rhinodermatidae		1	2	South America
Hylidae	Treefrogs	38	740	North America, Central America, South America, Europe, Asia, Africa, Australia, New Guinea
Pseudidae		2	4	South America
Centrolenidae	Glass frogs	3	120	Central America, South America
Microhylidae		65	315	North America, Central America, South America, Africa, Asia, Australia, New Guinea
Dendrobatidae	Poison dart frogs	6	175	Central America, South America
Hemisotidae	Shovel-nosed frogs	1	8	Africa
Arthroleptidae	Squeakers	7	75	Africa
Sooglossidae	Seychelles frogs	2	3	Seychelles Islands
Ranidae	"True" frogs	46	700	North America, Central America, South America, Africa, Europe, Asia, Australia
Hyperoliidae	Reed and lily frogs	19	230	Africa
Rhacophoridae		10	212	Africa, Asia, Indo-Pacific

* This huge family, which includes nearly 900 species, is represented throughout South America and Central America and into the southern United States. Almost every mode of life available to anurans can be found in this family. It is probable that taxonomists will revise this family as relationships among these many species become better understood.

INDEX